Diving into the unknown, a Greek athlete
departs this world for the next.

(from a fifth-century B.C. tomb painting)

INTO THE UNKNOWN

Solving Ancient Mysteries

By Brian Fagan

Prepared by
The Book Division
National Geographic Society
Washington, D.C.

INTO THE UNKNOWN
Solving Ancient Mysteries

By Brian Fagan

Published by
The National Geographic Society

Reg Murphy
President and Chief Executive Officer

Gilbert M. Grosvenor
Chairman of the Board

Nina D. Hoffman
Senior Vice President

Prepared by
The Book Division

William R. Gray
Vice President and Director

Charles Kogod
Assistant Director

Barbara A. Payne
Editorial Director and Managing Editor

Staff for this book

Tom Melham
Managing Editor

Martha C. Christian
Text Editor

Greta Arnold
Illustrations Editor

Cinda Rose
Art Director

Victoria Cooper
Senior Researcher

Susan A. Franques
Research Assistant

Carl Mehler
Senior Map Editor

Joseph F. Ochlak
Map Research

Louis J. Spirito, Martin S. Walz
Map Production

Richard S. Wain
Production Project Manager

Lewis R. Bassford
Production

Jennifer L. Burke
Illustrations Assistant

Peggy Candore, Kevin G. Craig,
Dale-Marie Herring
Staff Assistants

Manufacturing and Quality Control

George V. White
Director

John T. Dunn
Associate Director

Vincent P. Ryan, Gregory Storer
Managers

Polly P. Tompkins
Executive Assistant

Elisabeth MacRae-Bobynskyj
Indexer

*In this life-size reproduction of a Moche burial, a
warrior-priest of Sipán lies surrounded by funerary
finery and by sacrificial victims in cane coffins.*

*PREVIOUS PAGES: Hot-air balloon hovers above Egypt's
modern-day Qurna and Thebes's City of the Dead,
across the road from ancient temple granaries.*

*FOLLOWING PAGES: Maya glyphs on the walls of
Guatemala's Naj Tunich ("stone house" or "cave")
were obliterated by vandals after this photograph
was made; the glyphs remain undeciphered.*

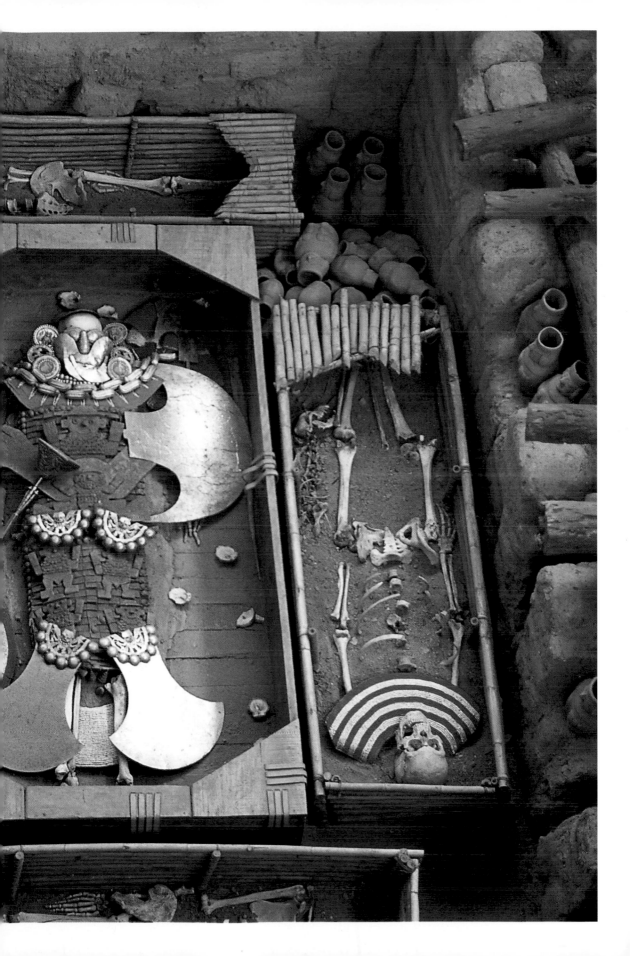

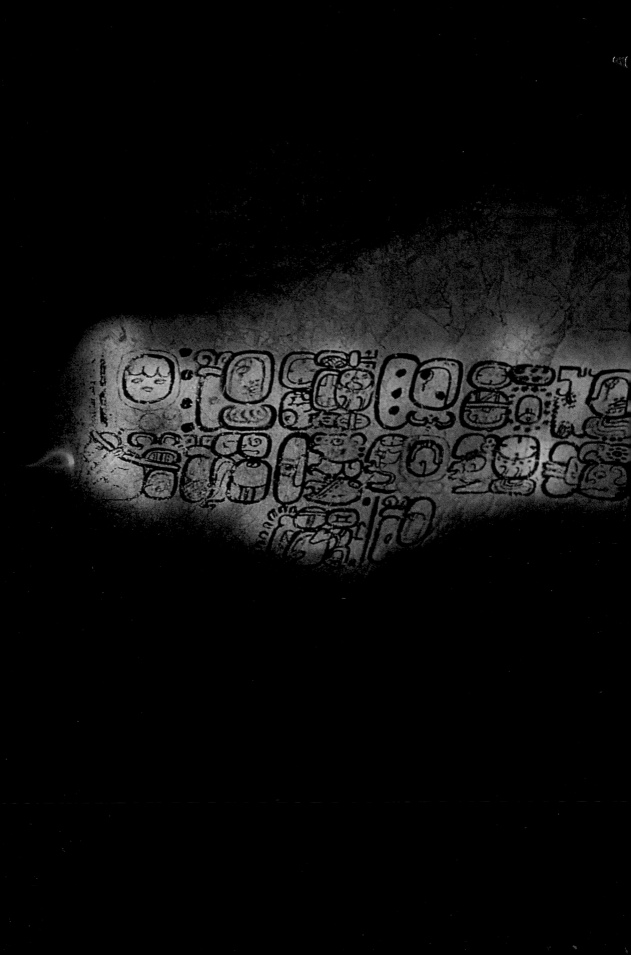

CONTENTS

INTRODUCTION   8

PEOPLE OF THE PAST   *16*

ANCIENT LANDSCAPES   *56*

WEBS OF COMMERCE   *90*

LIVES OF THE HUMBLE   *124*

MIRRORS OF THE INTANGIBLE   *150*

Index   194
Illustrations Credits   199
Author's Note, Additional Reading,
  and Acknowledgments   200

THE WORLD OF THE
PAST

Archaeology is the science of rubbish, the study of human societies through the surviving material remains of the past. Archaeologists are like people walking on a vast seashore gathering shells, except that their shells are stone tools and potsherds, food remains, house foundations, and the bones of the dead.

Often portrayed as Indiana Jones-like adventurers and pith-helmeted professors, archaeologists have been seen as romantic figures hard at work in remote, dangerous lands. Even three-quarters of a century ago, adventure and large-scale excavations went together. When British archaeologist C. Leonard Woolley excavated the Sumerian city of Ur in Mesopotamia, he presided over hundreds of workers toiling in the hot sun. Woolley was a general, deploying an archaeological army; he was

Archaeology a century ago: Endless line of diggers carries off overburden from ancient Sumer's religious center of Nippur during 1899 excavations. Nippur yielded clay tablets bearing tales of creation and a great flood.

one of the last heroic excavators, at a time when archaeologists still dug up entire cities and astounded the world with spectacular discoveries. His description of Sumerian Queen Puabi's funeral, at which members of the court filed into the burial pit, swallowed poison, and lay down in order of precedence to die, ranks among archaeology's classic discoveries.

The stereotype of the virile adventurer persists today, even in a changed archaeological world, one in which discoveries come as much in the air-conditioned laboratory as in the field.

All science is a product of its time. Today's archaeologists possess analytical tools so sophisticated that they can identify ancient strains of wheat from microscopic plant pollens, tell the direction of the wind during a bison hunt 8,000 years ago, and pinpoint the source of obsidian, volcanic glass, made into a Maya mirror. They use magnetometers to map Roman towns. They study the history of wine by chemically analyzing residues in clay storage pots. They employ computers to manipulate enormous amounts of data. For example, by digitizing and analyzing information about artifacts and site distributions, archaeologists discover how human settlement patterns have changed over thousands of years. They also use computers to produce three-dimensional models—such as long-vanished Egyptian temples in ancient Kush—and to reconstruct buildings such as those demolished by earthquake in the Roman port at Kourion, on Cyprus. With the aid of computers, archaeologists fill in lost features of the Sphinx and enhance faded murals at Bonampak, Mexico.

Archaeology was a tiny profession in the 1920s. Now there are thousands of archaeologists in Europe and North America, and nearly a hundred in South Africa alone. Egyptologists once numbered a few dozen. Today, hundreds of scholars, often with esoteric specialties, study ancient Egypt. Professionally directed excavations—some as salvage operations in advance of road construction or other development, some as purely scholarly digs—disturb more and more sites each year, but with a difference. Today's archaeologist takes a month or more to dig what Woolley's generation would have cleared in less than a week. Slow, meticulous, and managed by teams of scientists from many specialties, present-day excavations yield astoundingly fine-grained portraits of the past.

Into the Unknown visits archaeologists in the field and in the lab as they use new ways to study the past, ways that rely less on excavation and more on high technology. Our journey into the past focuses on five themes: people of the past, ancient landscapes, the interconnections of societies through trade, the daily lives of the humble, and the intangibles of human life—religious beliefs, art, storytelling, and such.

Pharaoh or commoner, 5,000-year-old mountaineer or 500-year-old Inupiat family, we are all equal in the face of death and medical science. "People of the Past" describes how archaeologists enlist pathology and forensic medicine to study ancient corpses. We know some of these individuals, such as Ötzi the Iceman from the Alps, better than they knew themselves—their injuries, their pathologies and parasites, even details of the last meals they ate. The occasional serendipitous find of someone who died suddenly in some long-forgotten tragedy places us alongside that person in his or her daily business. Thanks to the latest medical technology, we can sometimes look over the shoulders of the departed and establish where they came from or why they died.

"Ancient Landscapes" shows how new, nonintrusive methods allow us to explore the ways various societies have left their marks on the land. Probing beneath the ground's surface without excavating enables archaeologists to conserve finite site archives. Today's scientists have turned from tunneling and trenching burial mounds and cities to examining entire landscapes. Aerial archaeology, discussed in this chapter, embraces all kinds of photographic, digital imaging, and other technologies. Two examples: Radar imaging carried out by space shuttle revealed circular, mounded sites with vestiges of moats and earthworks at Angkor Wat in Cambodia; Geographic Information Systems (GIS) technology helped researchers map hitherto unknown buildings and other features of a Roman town at the site of present-day Wroxeter, England.

The glitter of polished gold and copper, the seductive lure of a soapstone vase, the brilliant sheen of a mirror fashioned from volcanic glass: People have craved the exotic and the precious since remote times. "Webs of Commerce" shows how archaeologists study ancient trade. Only a fraction of the evidence survives, sometimes in the form of gold ornaments, sometimes as glass beads or seashells. The distribution of such artifacts gives a general impression of ancient trade routes. But far more precise information comes from a new generation of sourcing methods that use spectrographic analysis to trace obsidian, copper, and other stones and metals back to their original sources. Sourcing comes into its own on those occasions when underwater archaeologists discover an undisturbed shipwreck such as the one found off Uluburun, Turkey. About 3,300 years old, it is a priceless repository of information. The ship carried a cargo that came from all over the eastern Mediterranean.

People's lives, however, involve more than the relatively impersonal transactions of the marketplace. They require constant negotiating with family members, friends, neighbors, and law enforcement and government authorities. In the past, archaeology has presented a homogeneous portrait of human societies. All too often we have looked at such societies only through the eyes of the rich, the literate, and the powerful. Commoners had no voice, except for the dispassionate and often revealing testimony of their artifacts. "Lives of the Humble" uses everyday objects to explore some of the complex social interactions of the past.

The study of the intangible may be the most challenging archaeology of all. Often, a fine line divides unbridled speculation from intelligent guesswork—which is based on solid evidence extracted from a precise context. "Mirrors of the Intangible" explores another frontier, where archaeologists grapple with fundamental questions of existence. This chapter deals with tangible remains—the mirrors—of once vibrant human societies. We cannot talk with long-vanished peoples, who lived in worlds incredibly different from our own. We can only guess at the elaborate rituals that unfolded deep in Stone Age caves, or the meaning of plaster statues from prehistoric 'Ain Ghazal, in Jordan. Fortunately, today's archaeologists are using architecture, art, and sometimes arcane sources to open dialogues with the intangible aspects of the ancient world.

Romance and adventure are still alive and well in archaeology, even if the focus has changed and the finds are often less spectacular than in earlier eras. And the miracles of science described in these pages hint that some of archaeology's greatest discoveries still lie ahead.

Memories of a once green land: A watchful archer stands ready as he stalks prey on a

sandstone wall at Tassili-n-Ajjer (Plateau of the Rivers), in the heart of the now arid Sahara. 13

Staring into eternity, restored single- and double-headed plaster figures dating to

6500 B.C. were found at 'Ain Ghazal, on the outskirts of Amman, Jordan.

PEOPLE
OF
THE PAST

in those of thousands of other archaic humans.... Her identity comes from an elusive genetic signature, from DNA..."

"And Adam called his wife's name Eve; because she was the mother of all...." The biblical Eve is the legendary first woman, a symbol of the beginnings of humankind.

Today, scientists speak of another Eve. She is a hypothetical construct, a product of molecular anthropology, the latest chapter in a long search for the first modern humans, people like us. This Eve is dark haired, well muscled, and black skinned, and she roamed the African savanna about 200,000 years ago.

She was a member of a small hunter-gatherer band, strong enough to carry heavy loads of fruits and nuts, and to tear apart animal flesh with her hands. She was not the only woman on earth, or the most beautiful, or even the one with the most children. But her genes are in every living human being.

Testament to human diversity in an increasingly mobile world, the sun-coppered face of this 12-year-old Tajik girl from Xinjiang, western China, reflects Indo-European rather than Mongoloid heritage.

All 5.8 billion of us today are her blood relatives. One scientist estimates that she is our 10,000th-great-grandmother.

Was there actually an African Eve, a woman of flesh and blood? We can never hope to identify her in person. Her identity is submerged in those of thousands of other archaic humans who lived in Africa at the time. Her identity comes from an elusive genetic signature, from DNA (deoxyribonucleic acid) she contributed to later generations that evolved into *Homo sapiens sapiens*.

Archaeologists have searched for our remotest ancestors ever since the discovery of a primitive-looking Neandertal skull in Germany in 1856. The Victorian biologist Thomas Henry Huxley compared the Neandertal cranium with those of archaic and modern humans and proclaimed it an ancestor of modern humanity. He wrote prophetically in his classic 1863 book, *Evidence as to Man's Place in Nature,* that evolution would "extend by long epochs the most liberal estimate that has yet been made of the antiquity of Man." Biologist Charles Darwin, of *Origin of Species* fame, pointed to Africa, with its great variety of apes, as the cradle of humankind.

How right Darwin and Huxley were! Nearly a century and a half later, molecular anthropology tells us that our closest living relatives, the chimpanzees, separated from the human line between five and seven million years ago. Paleontologist Tim White, of the University of California at Berkeley, has unearthed the bones of an apelike hominid at Aramis, in Ethiopia, that dates to 4.4 million years ago, close to that critical time.

A vast evolutionary chasm separates us from the earliest hominids. We are *Homo sapiens sapiens*, the clever person, an animal capable of subtle thought and self-understanding. Unlike our earliest ancestors, we speak in articulate tongues, reason intelligently, and have a sense of our own identity. But where and when did we originate? Did we evolve in one continent, or more or less simultaneously in Africa, Europe, and Asia? Herein lies one of the great controversies of archaeology.

Only a couple of generations ago, we knew fairly little about the immediate ancestors of *Homo sapiens sapiens*. A scattering of fragmentary fossil skulls and limb bones documented the rise of Neandertals and modern people from more archaic human forms. The oldest of these anatomically modern-looking finds included some from Border Cave and Klasies River Mouth, both in South Africa, and appeared to date to about 100,000 years ago. Many paleoanthropologists believed we had evolved on three continents simultaneously.

While they argued about fossils, molecular biologists probed the secrets of DNA, the physical basis of life. DNA contains the hereditary information to transform inanimate matter into living matter, to build new organisms. DNA directs the formation of our descendants. It is the substance that allows biological features to be handed down from one generation to the next.

Stanford University geneticist Luigi Luca Cavalli-Sforza calls the DNA needed to manufacture a single human a multivolume encyclopedia, with one volume for each of the 23 chromosomes in each of the two germinal cells. Cavalli-Sforza is a pioneer in human genetics, the study not of artifacts and food remains but of the genetic wellspring of life itself.

During the 1980s, Allan C. Wilson, of the University of California at Berkeley, began an intensive study of mitochondrial DNA. Mitochondria

Fleshed out with computers and human artistry, this male Australopithecus afarensis *probably stood five feet tall in life, at least a foot taller than females of the species. He and his kind flourished three million years ago in Africa, eventually evolving into diverse hominid populations, among them the first archaic human forms.*

The skull of this particular individual was discovered at Hadar, Ethiopia, in 1992 by scientists from the Institute of Human Origins, now located at Arizona State University. It was reassembled from nearly 60 fragments. Using computerized mirror imaging and stereolithography, scientists produced a three-dimensional model. Artist John Gurche then added plasticine muscles, fat, and skin to complete this re-creation.

are the tiny structures in each cell that supply the energy for metabolism.

With only 37 genes, mitochondrial DNA (mtDNA) is far less complex than nuclear DNA, which contains the 60,000 to 100,000 genes that make up a human genetic blueprint. But mitochondria—the structures containing mtDNA—occur not in the nucleus but in the cytoplasm, which comes only from the mother's ovum, not the father's sperm. Thus, mammals inherit their mtDNA strictly through the maternal line. It is this quirk of biology that allows molecular anthropologists to create genealogies that link the maternal lineages of modern human populations to ancient humans.

Diverse in some ways, remarkably similar in others, all modern humans stem from the same evolutionary twig. We have adjusted to extremes of elevation, climate, and other factors. Examples of current diversity include the Kung San people (above), whose wiry build is well suited to the hot, dry climate of southern Africa.

Bronze plaque of Mongol lord Genghis Khan (opposite, top) commemorates the conqueror's 13th-century campaigns, which changed Asia's genetic makeup by sparking numerous population shifts. Mongols are compact, well adapted to cold (opposite, bottom).

Development of the polymerase chain reaction (PCR) method in the late 1980s enabled scientists to generate unlimited copies of any DNA fragment. This method separates DNA's double helix into two single strands, then synthesizes complementary strands to produce two helices, each consisting of an original strand attached to a newly created one. Researchers can now duplicate even a single DNA fragment as many times as they want. The analytical procedures for studying mitochondrial DNA are simple enough today, involving extraction of DNA from a tissue sample and the use of PCR to copy a portion of it. The researcher then compares the DNA fragment to DNA sequences taken from other individuals or populations, to establish a genetic relationship.

In 1987 Allan Wilson, along with biochemists Rebecca L. Cann and Mark Stoneking, caused a sensation when they published a study of the mtDNA of 147 people from all over the world. They found that these mitochondrial DNA samples could be divided into 133 distinct types, allowing them to create a family tree linking the maternal lineages of modern human populations to a common but hypothetical ancestral female in sub-Saharan Africa. They identified Africa as the most likely source of the human mitochondrial gene pool because African populations had a much higher level of genetic diversity than non-Africans. This, they argued, was the result of a much longer period of genetic mutation for Africans than for less diverse populations. They calculated that 2 to 4 percent of human mtDNA mutates every million years.

The researchers also found that the mtDNA lineages that diverged from the original African Eve have changed by an average of nearly 0.57 percent. This implies that the ancestor of all surviving mtDNA types lived between 140,000 and 290,000 years ago. Wilson, Cann, and Stoneking estimated that the oldest human populations to leave Africa that have no modern African representation dated to between 90,000 and 180,000 years ago. They concluded that all modern humans originated in Africa.

Their study ignited a firestorm of controversy. While later research has confirmed the genetic diversity of African populations, scientists still disagree as to what it means. Does this greater genetic variation in Africa reflect a population that was much bigger than non-African populations in the past? Or was Africa the cradle both of the first humans and of the first modern people as well? For years, archaeologists have been divided on this issue. Some scholars believe that modern humans developed from earlier, more archaic peoples living in several regions, including Africa, Asia, and Europe.

Proponents of this "multiregional" hypothesis pit themselves against a much larger group of experts, who agree with Wilson, Cann, and Stoneking that modern humans evolved in sub-Saharan Africa, then spread out into Asia and Europe, replacing earlier human populations. Members of the out-of-Africa school point to the Klasies River Mouth fossils, still among the earliest anatomically modern humans known to be representative of the early humans that gave rise to us all. Molecular anthropology is a burgeoning field, one that has unlimited potential for examining our past. If the Wilson-Cann-Stoneking team is correct, then Africa was the cradle not only of humanity, but of modern humans as well.

Harvard University evolutionary biologist Stephen Jay Gould agrees with the out-of-Africa hypothesis, a striking and simple model of an evolutionary tree with two major branches joined at the base. He believes we are all products of the same evolutionary "twig." Despite our external differences of skin color, hair, form, and size, we all share a relatively recent common ancestry in Africa.

The molecular anthropologists have demonstrated the underlying unity of all humankind, a contingent fact of history with striking relevance to studying the people of the past.

"A generation passes, and another remains," sings an unnamed, ancient Egyptian harpist as he laments the transitory nature of human life. "No one returns from there to tell their conditions, their state." Many variations of this song appear on the walls of ancient Egyptian tombs, adjuring the living to make the most of life before they pass into "the land that loves silence," eternity.

Wealthy Egyptians long ago adorned their rock-cut sepulchres with orderly scenes of life on earth. In those ancient scenes, rightness, a sense of order, prevails. Agricultural workers labor in a nobleman's fields under the watchful eye of the ever present scribe. Stewards bring beef and fattened geese to the aristocratic table. Serving girls wait on smartly dressed ladies at a banquet. Egyptian tomb paintings present the world as it was supposed to be. Archaeology tells us reality was usually very different.

Although modern humans have lived on earth at least 100,000 years, the earliest written records—mainly commercial transactions—go back only about 5,000 years. Epic poems, lists of kingly successions, and historical documents that name names appear somewhat later, at first in eastern Mediterranean lands. Therefore, most of our past is anonymous, a history of group behavior reconstructed from art, durable artifacts, food remains, building foundations, and burials.

Like all excavators, I have often stood in the midst of a complicated dig wishing that I could have five minutes alone with the people who had once lived there, to listen to their individual stories, to learn of their complex dealings with one another and with society at large.

Now, thanks to accidents of preservation and to advances in modern medical science, we *can* sometimes meet individuals—kings, queens, and commoners alike. Our scientific "conversations" with them help us know them better than they perhaps knew themselves.

These conversations began more than a century ago, with a sensational discovery close to Egypt's Valley of the Kings. Thebes was a bustling town in the 1870s. Every winter, boatloads of American and European tourists moored near the ancient temples of Luxor and Karnak. Antiquities dealers flocked to the arriving boats. They offered scarabs and funerary statuettes, spirited from the depths of their flowing robes.

"They waylaid and followed us wherever we went; while some of the better sort—grave men in long black robes and ample turbans—installed themselves on our lower deck, and lived there for a fortnight," wrote British tourist Amelia B. Edwards.

The dealers did a roaring trade in genuine antiquities as well as in forgeries. They hawked forged scarabs that had been antiqued by passing them through a turkey's digestive system, from which they "acquire by the simple process of digestion a degree of venerableness that is really charming." Meanwhile, the tomb robbers quietly reserved their finest artifacts for experienced buyers and the agents of overseas museums.

In 1881 authorities heard rumors of exceptionally fine antiquities for sale, including jewelry bearing royal insignia. Soon the finger of suspicion pointed at a tomb-robbing family headed by the Abd el-Rassoul brothers of Qurna. Torture and beatings of the suspects produced no information, but eventually the family quarreled over the division of their spoils. One brother, Mohammed, then confessed to the chance discovery of a rocky cache full of magnificent grave furniture and mummies at Deir el-Bahari near the Valley of the Kings. For years the brothers had hidden their finds in their clothing or in baskets of vegetables and had smuggled them piece by piece into Luxor.

A few days after Mohammed's confession, Egyptologist Emil Brugsch descended on a long rope into the hiding place, a deep cleft. His candle shone on a cache of pharaohs. "And what Pharaohs!" wrote Gaston Maspero, director-general of the Service of Antiquities. "Perhaps the most illustrious in the history of Egypt, Thutmose III and Seti I, Ahmose the Liberator and Ramses II the Conqueror."

Around 1000 B.C., desperate priests had moved the mummies and the possessions of recently buried kings from one sepulchre to the next, to thwart voracious tomb robbers. Eventually the priests stacked generations of pharaohs in a remote cavern, where they would remain undetected for 3,000 years.

After Brugsch's discovery, some 300 workers carried the precious finds from the hiding place to a waiting government steamship on the Nile. In Cairo, Maspero and his colleagues eagerly unwrapped some of the royal mummies and gazed on the countenances of some of the ancient world's most powerful rulers. Seti I, a New Kingdom pharaoh, was the best preserved: a "fine kingly head," noted Maspero. He added, "A calm and gentle smile still played over his mouth."

In those days everyone enjoyed unwrapping mummies. Egyptologists would gather for a congenial lunch or dinner, then gather round the waiting corpse in eager anticipation. But the Deir el-Bahari cache with its unique royal mummies changed the rules. Because Seti I, Ramses II, and other pharaohs had been so powerful in their day, a few Egyptologists realized that the royal corpses were worth conserving as potential gold mines of information, not only as historical figures, but also as living and breathing people. What diseases had they suffered from? What had been their diets? Could one identify precise biological relationships between individual royal mummies?

New medical advances soon came to Egyptology's assistance. In 1895, German physicist Wilhelm Conrad Röntgen discovered the X ray, enabling scientists to look inside the human body without surgery. The great English Egyptologist Flinders Petrie, a pioneer of scientific excavation and analysis along the Nile, saw the historical potential at once. He made what may be the first X rays of mummies.

Anatomist and anthropologist Grafton Elliot Smith published a medical study of the royal mummies in 1912. In a memorable instance of scientific improvisation, Smith transported Pharaoh Tuthmosis IV's mummy to the cumbersome X-ray machine in a Cairo hospital by taxi!

By the time Howard Carter found Tutankhamun's tomb in 1922, a simple postmortem examination had become a routine part of unwrapping an Egyptian mummy.

Archaeology has come a long way since the first crude dissection of Tutankhamun's mummy, in 1923. Sophisticated X-ray imagery and other techniques such as CT (computed tomography) scanning allow us to explore even unwrapped mummies. Blood-group studies and chemical and physical analyses of soft tissues have proved to be powerful weapons, both in identifying royal mummies and in establishing the bloodline relationships among them—especially when combined with historical records of the Egyptians themselves. Today, the very latest high-technology diagnostics probe the ancient Egyptians' innermost medical secrets. For example, the 16th-century B.C. Pharaoh Seqenenre II was said to have died in battle. An X ray of his mummy revealed details of the terrible head wounds that likely killed him.

Sometimes X rays contradict history. Pharaoh Tuthmosis I, who ruled over Egypt from 1524 to 1518 B.C., died in middle age—according to historical sources. But X rays of the skeleton identified as his revealed features that indicate the mummified body had belonged to a young, still growing man, no older than 18 to 22. Many pharaohs were far from healthy men. Ramses II suffered from arteriosclerosis, clearly visible as arterial calcification in his carotid arteries and in images of his feet.

Mitochondrial DNA analysis, in particular, offers almost unlimited potential for studying alliances among ancient Egyptian rulers. A case in point: Egyptologists have long struggled with the genealogy of the New Kingdom pharaohs, who ruled Egypt between 1570 and 1070 B.C. Royal brothers and sisters, even fathers and daughters, often intermarried. What, for example, were the exact relationships between pharaohs and their immediate predecessors? Which of a pharaoh's wives was the mother of his heir? Historical identifications, either by original priestly records or by modern scholars working with mummies, were not necessarily reliable.

Neither were comparisons of skull measurements taken from X rays. DNA analysis of tissue samples from the mummies, however, offers a much better chance of discovering identities and deciphering relationships. Since 1993 Scott Woodward, of Brigham Young University, and Nasry Iskander, of the Egyptian Museum in Cairo, have been working in this field, analyzing mtDNA extracted from mummified New Kingdom kings and queens. Identifications often are difficult because the samples are tiny and because the perfumes and other substances used by the embalmers can make the tissue unsuitable for such analysis.

Woodward and Iskander face a challenging puzzle of marital relationships and parentage. For example, Ankhensenpaaten was the wife of Tutankhamun, and probably the mother of the two fetuses found in small, intricate, double-layered coffins in his tomb. She derived her mtDNA from her mother Nefertiti, wife of the heretic Pharaoh Akhenaten. If the fetuses prove to have the same mitochondrial DNA, then the likelihood of their being siblings is high. And if they were Ankhensenpaaten's

*M*ore than mere bone, fossils can tell us what a creature looked like, when it was alive, and even how closely it may be related to us. Casts of hominid fossils and chimp skulls help a team from the Institute of Human Origins (right) identify an Australopithecus afarensis *jaw from Ethiopia. Single-laser-fusion dating (bottom right) uses a laser beam to release argon gas from feldspar crystals in fossil-bearing rock. Since argon accumulates at*

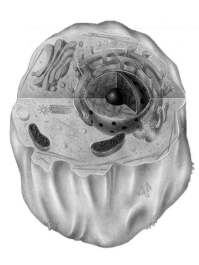

known rates, the amount released reveals the age of the rock—and thus of the fossils.

Human cells (left) carry DNA primarily in the nucleus (purple), but also in the cell proper, within mitochondria (red). Unlike nuclear DNA, which comes from both parents, mtDNA is inherited only from the mother. Thus, by analyzing tissues or fossils, researchers can trace ancient maternal lineages and deduce migration patterns.

children, then their mtDNA might also match that of the mummy from Tomb 55, which some believe to be Nefertiti.

Quite aside from the privileged existence of the royal families and high officials who ruled Egypt, thousands of Egyptian commoners lived in towns and rural villages. The mummified remains of these humble folk await detailed study. But we already know that their bodies paint a sobering picture of short life expectancies and harsh daily existences in the land of the pharaohs.

Recently, Egyptologists have developed methods of measuring bones on-site with X rays, combining this approach with studies of mummified tissues, including DNA analysis. This allows them to study entire cemetery populations rather than isolated bodies in museums. For example, two adults and a child found in a commoners' cemetery in the Faiyum Oasis southwest of Cairo—dating to between 300 B.C. and A.D. 400—have been shown, by analyzing mtDNA and nuclear DNA, to be members of a single family who were buried together.

Commoners' cemeteries throughout the Nile Valley are a litany of medical pathologies. Infant mortality rates were high. Those who survived past infancy could look forward to an average age of 40 years. Egyptians ate a coarse bread with a sand content high enough to wear down the crowns of their teeth, often causing gum damage and abscesses.

In 1976, French archaeologist Serge Sauneron, director of the Institut Français d'Archéologie Orientale in Cairo, began digging at Duch, a village in the extreme south of the Kharga Oasis, in the Libyan Desert west of the Nile. Duch was occupied between 100 B.C. and A.D. 400, during the heyday of Roman Egypt. At least 5,000 people lived in the village at its apogee; theirs was a remote community where old Egyptian cultural and religious traditions endured long after they had vanished along the Nile.

Françoise Dunand, of the University of Strasbourg, excavated the village necropolis, uncovering more than 700 skeletons or mummified bodies. J. L. Heim, from the Musée de l'Homme, and Roger Lichtenberg, director of radiology at the Institut Arthur Vernes in Paris, studied the remains. They measured the bones as all archaeologists do, but they also decided to X-ray the mummies with the aid of a portable machine hooked up to an on-site electric generator, in order to obtain a complete cross section of the village population.

First they cleaned the mummies of sand encrustations, so that artifacts would not appear on the X rays. Next they developed a clinical description of each corpse, took photographs for comparative measure-ments, and then shot at least eight X rays of all parts of the body, paying special attention to the skull. In some cases the researchers took samples of hair, nails, skin, resin, and embalming products for laboratory analysis before placing the mummies in well-protected tombs.

Based on this research, Dunand, Lichtenberg, and Heim developed an extraordinary portrait of the Duch people. The villagers turned out to be of Mediterranean physical type, slender, and of average height. The men stood about five feet four inches tall, the women about five one. They had pale skin and dark hair, like most ancient Egyptians. Without taking into account the very high infant mortality rate, the average life span was 38 years. Many of the Duch people had developed osteoarthritis and scoliosis, conditions linked to hard agricultural labor and the carrying of heavy loads. The drudgery and repetitiveness of their labors had left telling imprints on their bones.

Almost two-thirds of the sample population displayed stress lines on their bones that had resulted from episodes of malnutrition. Called Harris lines, after the medical researcher who first noted their occurrence, they can be seen in X rays of human long bones. They develop whenever metabolic stress causes cartilage recession and arrests bone growth.

X rays and clinical observations also revealed that one child died of typhoid, another from a fractured skull, and an old woman from a broken thigh. The lesions characteristic of parasitic diseases, such as filariasis and bilharzia, were present. Like many other humble folk in the ancient world, the Duch farmers endured lives of physical deprivation and hard labor, without benefit of medical care. Thus, human skeletons and mummies are often the medical records of the past, dispassionately revealing the consequences of years of backbreaking work—and of the division of labor between men and women.

Bones also have proved capable of telling the stories of ancient people who lived on the Euphrates River in what is now northern Syria. In 1972 and 1973 archaeologist Andrew M. T. Moore, of the University of Oxford, dug a large occupation mound at Abu Hureyra, which had begun as a small hunter-gatherer settlement of pit dwellings built between 9500 and 8000 B.C. At that time, the settlement occupied a well-watered, grassy steppe, near open woods where the inhabitants could hunt migrating gazelles every spring. They also gathered nuts, fruits, and seeds, including wild wheat, rye, and barley. Abu Hureyra prospered until between 300 and 400 people lived on the growing mound. Then, for unknown reasons, the site was abandoned.

Some two centuries later, a quite different village arose on that mound. This was a closely knit community of rectangular, one-story mud-brick houses joined by narrow alleys and courtyards. At first the inhabitants hunted gazelles intensively, as their predecessors had. But within a generation or two, about 7700 B.C., they switched to growing pulses, einkorn, and other cereals. Herding of domesticated sheep and goats was adopted about 6300 B.C.

Moore's meticulous excavations revealed much about the settlement of one of the earliest farming communities in the world, including the many permutations it had gone through over thousands of years. In the process, Moore also gave other researchers an opportunity to study individual inhabitants. During his digs he recovered the skeletal remains of what apparently were 162 residents from Abu Hureyra: 75 children and 87 adults, 44 of which were female, 27 male, the rest of undetermined sex.

Paleontologist Theya Molleson, of the Natural History Museum in London, realized these bones and teeth would reveal much about daily life at Abu Hureyra. She soon discovered that the general health of the people had been good, except for bone deformities caused by demanding, repetitive tasks. For example, some adolescents had enlarged parts on the vertebrae of their necks. These critical bones had developed a buttressing support for heavy loads carried on the head.

Molleson also found signs of stress on the last thoracic vertebra, and knees with bony extensions on their articular surfaces. Many Abu Hureyra people had enlarged toe joints and gross arthritic conditions of the big toe. She was at a loss to explain her observations of the leg and toe bones until a colleague visiting Egypt noticed that kneeling supplicants depicted on the walls of temples always had their toes curled forward. This simple observation led Molleson to speculate that an activity involving kneeling might be responsible for the pathologies she had observed. She knew, for example, that long hours of grinding grain had been the most time-consuming activity in the village. Archaeologists had found querns—bottom grinding stones—directly on the ground in the houses, so the individuals who ground the grain would have had to kneel for long periods.

Eventually, Molleson reconstructed the grinding process: The grinder put grain on the quern and gripped the grinding stone with both hands. Kneeling with toes bent, he or she then pushed the stone forward, arms turning inward as the stone moved to the end of the quern. As the upper body became so extended that it was almost parallel to the floor, the worker jerked the stone back.

Molleson also found that many of the Abu Hureyra arm bones had supported well-developed arm muscles. The last thoracic vertebra of many individuals displayed signs of disk damage and crushing, probably caused by repeating the back-and-forth movements too quickly or vigorously. The body pivoted around the knee and hip joints, which placed considerable bending stress on the thigh bones and deformed them. Many toe bones showed characteristic signs of cartilage damage and osteoarthritis resulting from kneeling many hours.

Did men or women grind the Abu Hureyra grain? Molleson took measurements of the first metatarsal bone of the foot. The larger, male bones showed little wear. In contrast, the shorter, female metatarsals displayed signs of heavy wear. Thus she believes that, at Abu Hureyra, grain was prepared by women and girls in a loose division of male and female roles. The men hunted and did the heavy agricultural labor, while women shouldered the laborious work of preparing food. As a result they suffered repetitive-stress injuries.

Even more insights would result from examining the Abu Hureyra skeletons. The coarsely ground grain, with its small stones and hard kernels, fractured and wore down people's teeth almost to the gums—findings related to those made at the Egyptian village of Duch. A scanning electron microscope helped Molleson find pits in the Abu Hureyra teeth, pits that were comparable to those occurring in the teeth of modern apes and monkeys, due to date stones and other hard objects.

Several female jaws at the site had grossly enlarged joints and extremely uneven wear of the teeth: Lower teeth were abraded on the outside; upper teeth on the inside. Tying these findings to research conducted in the 1960s by Jesse D. Jennings, of the University of Utah, at Utah's Danger Cave, Molleson is almost certain that Abu Hureyra women made mats in a way similar to a procedure discovered in Utah. Jennings described numerous quids at his site that had been chewed by heavily worn teeth; in the same levels, he found pieces of cord made of chewed bulrush stems, as well as mats bound with the same type of cord.

Occasionally, long-forgotten tragedies provide archaeologists with unusual snapshots of the lives of individual families. One stormy night centuries ago, two Inupiat women—one in her 40s, the other in her 20s—

Signpost to the past, radiocarbon dating has been used for decades to deduce the ages of ancient people and their organic artifacts. Now, a new wrinkle: accelerator mass spectrometry (AMS) radiocarbon dating, which provides more accurate dates from smaller samples. It counts carbon-14 atoms by pulling them through a linear accelerator. AMS technology allows archaeologists to radiocarbon-date samples as small as individual seeds and as old as 40,000-50,000 years.

and three children slept in a small driftwood-and-sod house overlooking the Arctic Ocean at Utqiagvik, now part of Barrow, Alaska. Harsh subzero winds swept over the bluff. High waves sent sea ice crashing against the shore. Suddenly, tons of ice chunks surged over a protective ridge and fell on the house, crushing both the roof and the inhabitants. Neighbors left the collapsed dwelling alone, later salvaging some food and the upright timbers projecting through the ice. The lasting refrigeration of permafrost preserved the buried family intact for perhaps five centuries.

In 1982 Albert A. Dekin, Jr., of Binghamton University, State University of New York, was in Barrow excavating ancient houses of Utqiagvik. Relic hunters nearby were digging into an eroding bluff edge, and one of them brought Dekin a frozen human cranium with black hair adhering to it. Archaeologists and the local magistrate were soon on the scene. At the bluff they found human bones and a frozen, desiccated, tightly flexed body with the hair and most of the flesh intact. The magistrate had the corpse placed in the morgue, as it appeared to be within her jurisdiction.

Several weeks later, other relic collectors uncovered another frozen body, this one inside a traditional Inupiat house, surrounded by artifacts and skins. Soon archaeologists Greg Reinhardt, Dale Slaughter, and Raymond R. Newell undertook a month's excavation of the house. The excavation was technically difficult, for the body and fragile artifacts had to be recovered before they thawed. Squirting warm water from bottles and chiseling away the ice matrix, the diggers worked day and night to remove the still-frozen body. They uncovered a remarkable time capsule of traditional Inupiat life.

The body turned out to be that of a woman in her 40s. The ruins of the Utqiagvik house were well preserved, the contents literally frozen in time. Eleven driftwood planks formed the floor of the rectangular dwelling, with plank walls and a timber-and-sod roof. A sleeping platform lay at the rear of the house, where the skeletons of three children came to light. The woman's body lay in front of the main beam of the house in a supine position, her upper body on a pile of clothing. Her left arm clutched a caribou-fur sleeping robe, which covered her. Her right arm covered her throat and shoulder in what might have been a reflex movement to protect herself from the collapsing roof.

The tightly flexed body, the one found first, proved to be that of a woman in her late 20s. The physicians who autopsied her found traces of a down robe or blanket adhering to her back. Like the older woman, she had been sleeping naked, perhaps to prevent moisture buildup. Had they worn their daytime garments to bed, any accumulated moisture would have frozen whenever the women went outside.

After all bodies and skeletons were out of the ground, they were flown to Fairbanks and autopsied by a team of medical scientists, with the permission of the Barrow elders. The bodies provided fascinating insights into the hazards of Arctic living. Physicians Michael R. Zimmerman and Arthur C. Aufderheide reported that the older woman had been lactating. She apparently had given birth two to six months earlier, but there were no signs of an infant in the house. The bladders of both women were distended, their stomachs empty, their colons partially full. These indicators pointed to the probability that both women had died in the early morning hours. Although generally in good health, both bodies showed signs of anthracosis, a condition equivalent to coal miners' black lung disease. In their case, the anthracosis resulted from inhalation of soot from seal-oil lamps within enclosed spaces, a common affliction among people living in poorly ventilated houses heated by open fires.

They also suffered from atherosclerosis and severe osteoporosis. In addition, malnutrition apparently had left the telltale marks of Harris lines on their bones. The older woman's body showed signs that she had survived diseases such as pneumonia, and possibly trichinosis.

In 1983 the archaeologists returned to the house to excavate its entry tunnel. They drilled soil borings, searching for a core with "clear ice" that revealed the tunnel cavity. The tunnel itself was a trench dug into the permafrost, roofed with wood and whale ribs that had been covered in turn with sod. Piles of more sod formed partitions that created alcoves, storage areas, and a kitchen. The alcoves contained skin bags full of clothing, artifacts, food storage containers, and raw materials. But there was almost no food, nor any stone lamps. Dekin believes that someone—quite possibly the males of the house—entered the tunnel, perhaps in the springtime after the disaster, and removed food and some utensils—despite an Inupiat belief that the houses of the dead should be left well alone.

Clearly the ice surge had buried the sleeping household of two women and three children. But where was the male hunter, perhaps the husband of the older woman, whose possessions had remained in the house? Had he been off visiting a relative? Had he been out on a winter hunting expedition? Or did he perish in the disaster in such a way that his body decayed, leaving no recoverable remains centuries later?

We do not know. Interestingly, his outdoor clothing was missing, whereas a woman's caribou parka, mittens, and waterproof sealskin boots lay in the entrance tunnel. Yet he had left many of his things in the house, including a bird-skin bag containing bone arrow points, a pair of shaft straighteners for making arrows, snow goggles, and round pebbles for bolas used to hunt waterfowl.

Most people of the past who come down to us as recognizable individuals are either exceptionally well-preserved burials or people killed in their homes by natural disasters. Some have been sacrificial victims.

Only rarely and under exceptional geological conditions can we study men or women of the past on the move, going about their daily business, their bodies preserved for centuries by the fortunate accident of extreme aridity or cold. To discover a 5,000-year-old prehistoric traveler who perished crossing a mountain pass almost exceeds the bounds of archaeological expectation. But just that happened in the Alps in September 1991, when German mountaineers Helmut and Erika Simon found what has become widely known as Ötzi the Iceman. The two were descending from a high alpine peak, just inside Italy along the Austrian border, and were making their way around a narrow gully near Hauslabjoch, at an elevation of 10,530 feet above sea level.

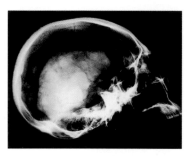

Suddenly Erika spotted something brown projecting from the ice and glacial meltwater in the base of the gully. At first she and Helmut thought it was merely a doll, but they soon identified the leather-brown skull, shoulders, and back as parts of a man, his face lying in water. The Simons assumed they had stumbled across a victim of a climbing accident, took a photograph of their find, then reported it to authorities.

The first police on the scene also assumed that they were dealing with a modern casualty. They tried to free the body, but the weather turned bad. They collected a wooden-handled copper ax lying alongside the corpse. This find prompted a larger police team to investigate.

With rough-and-ready improvisation that would later set the hair of archaeologists on end, the investigators first hacked open the ice around the man's buttocks and thighs with a jackhammer. On their next visit, they probed with ski poles and an ice pick. Finally, as they gradually eased the body out of the ice, the weather again deteriorated, so they hastily stuffed the still-frozen remains and a scattering of artifacts into a body bag, breaking off what turned out to be a wooden bow stave that projected from the ice. A few hours later, a unique archaeological discovery became corpse number 91/619 on the local forensic dissection table.

One can hardly blame the police for their handling of the body. After

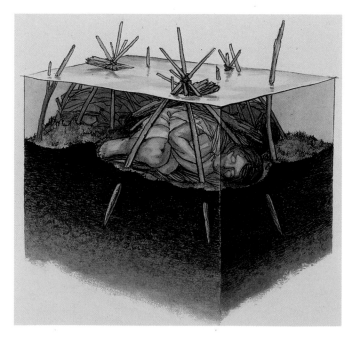

all, who would have expected to find a 5,000-year-old man 10,530 feet high in the Alps? None of the investigators were archaeologists possessing first-hand familiarity with archaeological artifacts. They treated the find as a possible accident or murder victim. A public prosecutor attended the preliminary examination, saw that the body was perhaps ancient, and authorized a phone call to archaeologist Konrad Spindler, of the University of Innsbruck. Within days, teams of scientists were at work on the find.

Archaeologists Andreas Lippert, of the University of Vienna, and Hans Nothdurfter, of the South Tyrol Ancient Monuments Office, organized follow-up excavations at the site, which by the beginning of October was already under two feet of new snow. They shoveled away what they could, then used a steam blower and hair dryer to recover part of a grass cloak, leaves, tufts of grass, and wood fragments. They established that a fully clothed Ötzi had deposited his ax, bow, and backpack on a ledge. He had lain down on his left side, his head on a boulder, perhaps taking shelter from the weather in the small gully. Judging from his relaxed limbs, the exhausted man had gone to sleep and had frozen to death a few hours later.

That the body of Ötzi was preserved is a miracle. Fortunately for science, he seems to have died at the end of autumn. Perhaps a thin layer of snow quickly covered his body, saving him from carrion-eaters and allowing natural mummification to proceed. Just as fortuitous was the gully in which the Iceman lay, for it eventually sheltered his body from the glacier that slowly flowed over the land. Five thousand years passed before a thaw in 1991 exposed the body, probably no more than a few days before its discovery. Just three days after Ötzi's body had been removed, the site was once again covered with snow.

Spindler knew from the ax and other artifacts that Ötzi was several thousand years old. Within a few weeks, grass fragments from the shoulder cape and some particles of bone and tissue fibers from the man's hip arrived at five laboratories in the United States, Britain, France, Sweden and Switzerland. Using accelerator mass spectrometry radiocarbon dating, the five dated Ötzi to between 3350 and 3120 B.C.

The Innsbruck research team faced a herculean task of conservation and a fascinating ancient mystery. First, medical experts assessed the body, relying on noninvasive methods. They immediately noticed groups of tattoos—mostly parallel vertical lines—adorning the Iceman's lower back, left calf, and right ankle. Three biological anthropologists from Vienna, Mainz, and Stockholm measured the skeleton and estimated that Ötzi had stood about 5 feet 2 inches tall and had been between the ages of 35 and 40 when he died. Later research indicated that he actually might have been as old as 47. He was well within the norms for contemporary prehistoric populations. X rays and CT scans provided information on the morphology of the corpse. The CT scans also revealed that Ötzi was probably hungry and weak at the time of death.

Austrian anthropologists examined his jaws and his very worn teeth, while Italian colleagues started work on his paleopathology. A team of molecular biologists took tissue samples from the left hip under sterile conditions. When Oliva Handt of the University of Munich analyzed the samples, she found mtDNA sequences different from other human sources. The left hip had been contaminated by handling during recovery efforts. Fortunately, two samples were large enough to allow removal of the contaminating layers. The Iceman's mtDNA sequence resembled that of modern alpine and northern Europeans.

Using specially designed titanium instruments that would leave no trace elements, a team headed by anatomist Werner Platzer of the University of Innsbruck took minute samples from Ötzi's organs and tissues. The samples were sent to scientists in Europe and the United States for analysis, to help assess the Iceman's general state of health and cause of death. Platzer found that the man's stomach was empty, but his large intestine contained considerable amounts of material.

Genetic gold mine, this shrunken, 7,000-year-old brain of a middle-aged woman (top) emerged from the preservative, pH-neutral waters of a Florida peat bog. It yielded what may be the oldest known human DNA yet found in the Americas. Microbiologists are trying to clone that DNA to learn more about the woman's ancestry. She belonged to a hunter-gatherer band that buried their dead in a foot-deep pond, often laying the bodies on their sides in flexed position (bottom). A branch framework secured each peat-covered grave.

Ötzi perhaps had not been in very good health. Environmental archaeologist Andrew Jones, of the Archaeological Resource Centre in York, England, studied samples of the Iceman's colon microscopically and identified the minute eggs of a parasitic whipworm. As yet, he has been unable to tell how severe the infestation was, but we know that even moderate cases can be debilitating.

Microbiologist Raúl J. Cano, of the California Polytechnic State University in San Luis Obispo, isolated DNA from a fungus named *Aspergillus,* found in the Iceman's lungs. *Aspergillus* has been associated with lung disease, but such a condition probably did not kill him. Neither did his smoke-blackened lungs, which were as discolored as those of a habitual smoker. Like the Utqiagvik women, he probably had lived in a small dwelling with an open hearth.

Cano also examined Ötzi's digestive system, which proved to contain "a full complement of 'modern' microbial flora." In addition, he discovered a potential waterborne pathogen called *Vibrio metschnikovii,* one sign that the Iceman had drunk fecally contaminated water.

Many indicators point to Ötzi's having lived a difficult life. When Horst Seidler, a biological anthropologist at the University of Vienna, examined X rays of the Iceman's shinbone, he found no less than 17 Harris lines, possibly indicating periods of severe dietary deficiencies, which occurred in Ötzi's 9th, 15th, and 16th years. A single surviving fingernail showed signs of hard manual labor and episodes of reduced growth, another clear sign of illness or dietary stress.

Archaeologist Don Brothwell, of the University of York, and physicist Geoffrey Grime, of the University of Oxford, measured unusually high amounts of copper on the surface of the Iceman's hair; they wonder whether Ötzi was involved in the processing of copper. So far, they have not examined the fingers and lungs for signs of telltale malachite dust, a copper carbonate that occurs naturally in some outcrops in the Alps. The Iceman carried no digging tools, and might have acquired the dust by sharpening his copper-bladed ax and then rubbing his hair with his hands.

When Ötzi died, he was fully clothed and carried various pieces of equipment fashioned from 17 wood and other plant materials; 8 species of animals made up the skins and animal products used in his clothing and tools. Many of the saturated and half-frozen pieces of clothing and artifacts had been shredded or damaged during the recovery of the body. As a result, conservation experts under the direction of Markus Egg, at the Roman-Germanic Central Museum in Mainz, Germany, faced an appallingly difficult puzzle. They did manage to achieve miracles of conservation that enabled them to reconstruct the Iceman's clothing.

On his last day alive, Ötzi wore as an undergarment a leather belt that doubled as a waist pouch. This contained three flint instruments and a bone awl, along with a mass of dry fungus and iron pyrite that functioned as tinder. The belt held up a leather loincloth. Suspenders led from the belt to a pair of fur leggings.

The Iceman also had on a coat made of alternating strips of black and brown animal skin. An outer cape of twisted grass covered the coat, a type of garment still used in the Alps up to the beginning of this century. A conical bearskin cap with the fur to the outside fastened below his chin with a strap. On his feet the Iceman wore bearskin and deerskin shoes filled with grass held in place by an inner string "sock."

Everything gives the impression of a self-sufficient individual with an array of skills. Ötzi clearly had been on the move, carrying a backpack attached to a wood frame, startlingly similar in design to those used in the mountains today. He also carried a sheathed flint dagger, a copper-bladed ax with a wooden handle, an rough longbow of yew, and a skin quiver filled with 14 arrows—12 of them unfinished. In addition, he had antler points and what may be bowstring material. He even carried two chunks of birch fungus, similar to fungi used today by folk doctors for their antibiotic properties. Each had been threaded on a separate leather thong.

It is possible that Ötzi climbed into the mountains from the south. He had probably been in a farming village a few days before he died, as two grains of wheat had lodged in his fur garments.

To this day, shepherds graze their sheep high in the Alps near where Ötzi perished. Was he also a shepherd, on his way to or from high-altitude summer pastures? Konrad Spindler believes the skins used to make the Iceman's coat are domesticated goat, and argues that he was a goatherd. But Ötzi carried no shepherd's equipment with him.

Was he a copper worker, searching for metal? Was he high in the mountains on a religious pilgrimage or quest? Was he hunting mountain goats? We do not know.

The Iceman's new home is a special freezer at the University of Innsbruck, set at minus 6°C (21°F) and equipped with a high-humidity feature to mimic glacial conditions. Any scientist who works on the body has only 20 to 30 minutes, including wrapping and unwrapping time, before the corpse must be put back. Everyone must wear sterile surgical outfits. Such precautions serve to protect this amazing individual of the distant past for discoveries that may be possible only in the future, generations from now.

Again and again, time has proved that today's tools of science will be improved tomorrow, enabling breakthroughs of knowledge not yet even dreamed of by today's sharpest minds. Pushing the limits of investigation and cooperation, an international mix of nearly 150 scientists from many disciplines have examined Ötzi's remains and artifacts. Such research epitomizes the sophisticated joining of forces that is required of modern archaeology. With the tools of all sciences conjoined to solve the mysteries of people of the past, these shadowy figures begin to take shape and come alive.

For the present, numerous questions persist about Ötzi the Iceman: Why was he so high in the Alps? Why did he die? Despite all we have learned so far, many circumstances of his death remain a mystery.

We again experience the haunting echo of the Egyptian harpist:

"A generation passes, and another remains. No one returns from there to tell their conditions, their state."

Ah, but perhaps some do. Tomorrow's archaeologists will doubtless have access to increasingly sophisticated investigative tools, and so will be able to communicate more fully with people of the past. They may find a more fitting quote in the words of the Apostle Paul, who, while commenting on the gradual illumination of the human mind, wrote:

"For now we see through a glass, darkly; but then face to face...."

aking a new look at an old misconception, the Neanderthal Museum in Erkrath, Germany, displays its namesake subject not as a clumsy brute but as just another "suit" (right). Science once dismissed Neandertals as distant relatives but now considers these 30,000- to 250,000-year-old hominids contributors to the modern human family.

Flowstone shrouds a fossilized Neandertal skeleton discovered in an Italian cave in 1993 (below). Increasingly, scientists rely on computers and other high-tech methods

to rebuild fossils. In Zurich, Swiss researchers replicated the fragmentary skull of one Neandertal child through CT scans and 3-D software. A computer-guided laser (below) hardens layers of plastic resin in the shape of the skull's cross sections.

Using software originally designed to artificially age pictures of missing children, Paul Neumann (opposite, bottom) at the University of Illinois at Chicago created digitized images of a model's face (opposite, top left) and

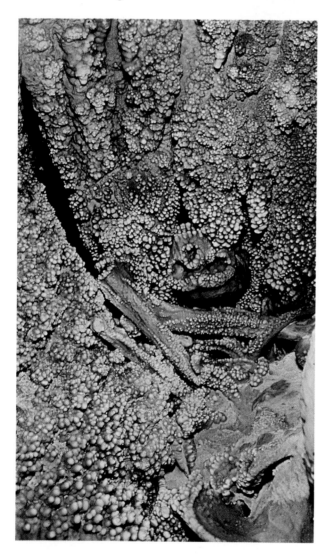

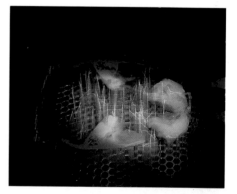

a female Neandertal skull (opposite, top center). His computer then "morphed" the face to fit the skull, creating a realistic "virtual Neandertal" (opposite, top right).

 canning mummies for clues: Ramses II, mightiest of pharaohs, epitomizes ancient Egypt at the height of its power. He was born during Egypt's golden age, in about 1303 B.C. He ruled for 67 years, living into his 90s. Early in his reign, teams of workers began to dig his rock-cut tomb in the Valley of the Kings, on the

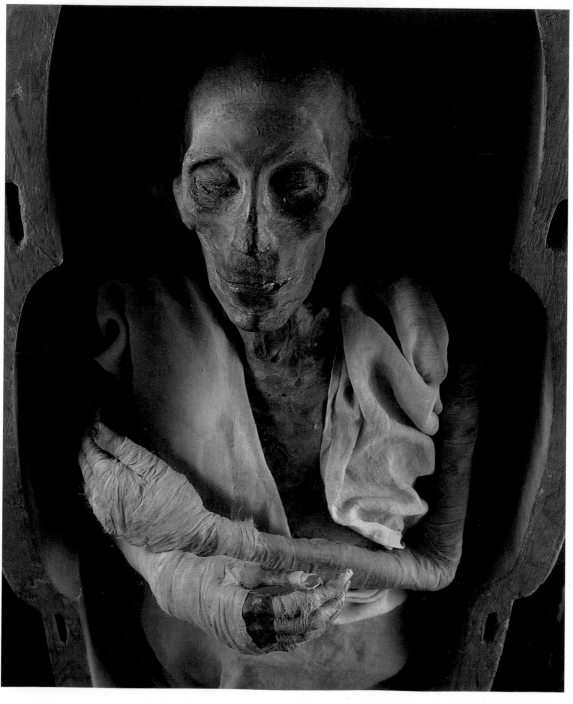

*west bank of the Nile, at
Thebes. Elaborate bas-reliefs
at the entrance (opposite, top)
welcomed Ramses to eternity
and praised the sun god in his
more than 70 forms. Priests
hid the body in a secret cleft
long ago, after looters violated
the royal tomb.*

*Found in 1881, the mummy
(opposite, bottom) suffered
deterioration before French
conservators succeeded in
stabilizing it in 1976. The
skeleton is that of a man
about five feet eight inches
tall, with a strong jaw and
nose. X rays show that Ramses
was afflicted with arthritis,
dental abscesses, and poor
circulation. Egyptian
mummies are so valuable
that researchers now use the
latest medical technologies to
study them, without removing
layers of cloth or damaging
mummified tissues.*

*Still in its sarcophagus, the
3,000-year-old mummy of a
woman named Ta-Bes enters
a CT scanner (below). The
resulting image configures
not only bones but also skin
and organs in arbitrary colors
(right). Blotches over the
heart and abdomen indicate
amulets worn to protect the
deceased from evil.*

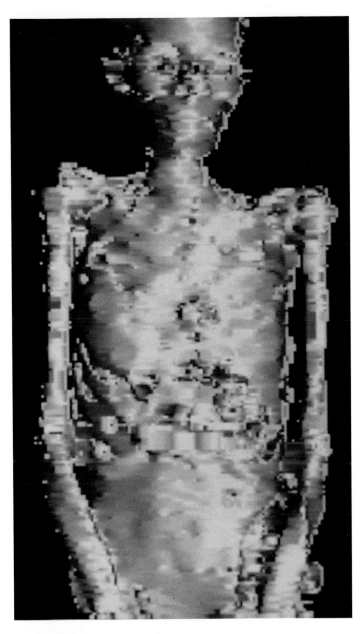

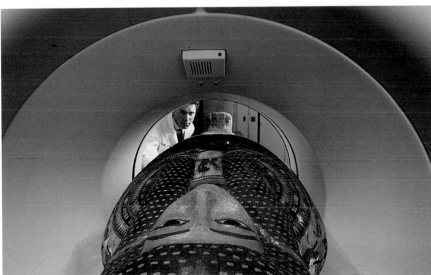

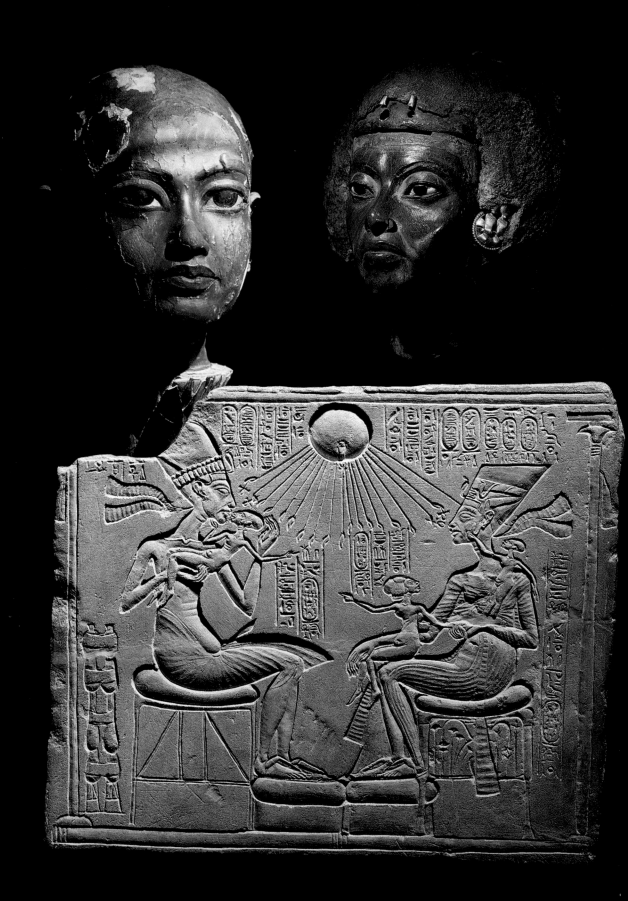

W*ho begat whom? When it comes to the royal families of ancient Egypt, contemporary portraiture often offers clues. But it can't supply all the answers, so scientists may turn to DNA studies to help clarify disputed blood lines. The young Tutankhamun (opposite, top left) is a genealogical enigma. He may have been the*

son of King Akhenaten, whose mother, the dowager Queen Tiy (opposite, top right) seems to share physical likeness with Tut. In relief, Akhenaten and his queen Nefertiti play with their three daughters (opposite, bottom). Inscriptions identify family members. Akhenaten was a heretic king who encouraged unorthodox

religious beliefs and more naturalistic art styles, epitomized by this unfinished bust of legendary beauty Nefertiti (left), "fair of face… great of love."

Artwork, hieroglyphs, and official records are only a prelude to other research. The 20-year-old daughter of a high priest (above) died in about 220 B.C. and was placed in a wooden coffin, with a child's mummy at her feet. DNA studies should reveal their relationship.

Ever at the ready, 2,200-year-old clay soldiers lead a horse-drawn chariot, all part

of a life-size terra-cotta army entombed with China's first emperor, Qin Shihuang.

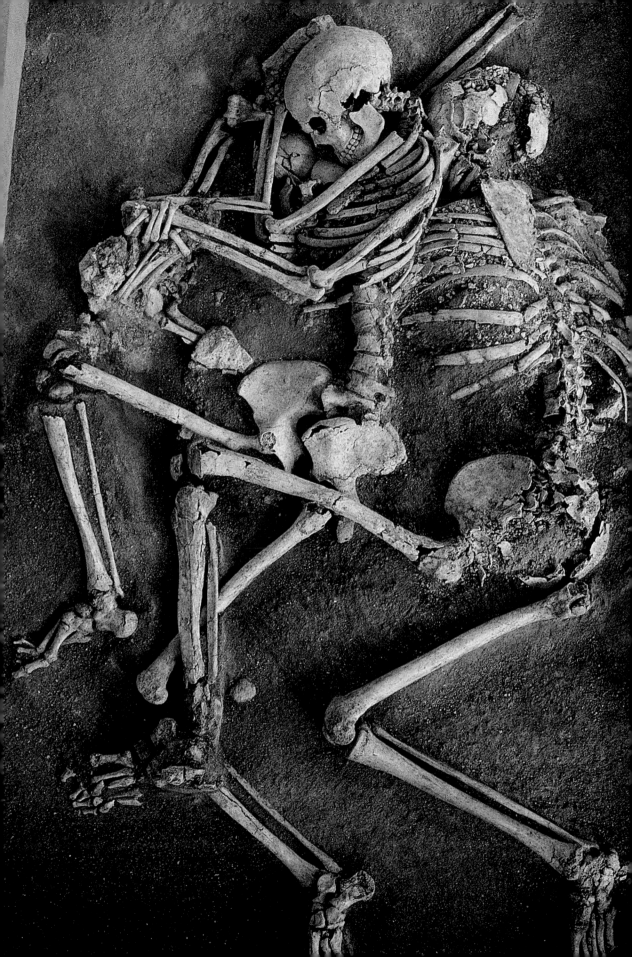

rapped in bed by an early morning earthquake 1,600 years ago, skeletal remains of a family (opposite) in southwestern Cyprus tell a tale of disaster. The 19-year-old mother still clutches her one-and-a-half-year-old child to her breast, while her 28-year-old husband vainly tries to shield them from a crushing rain of beams and limestone blocks. A quick

4:52:25

4:52:18

CYPRUS
KOURION
EPICENTER

4:51:07

MEDITERRANEAN SEA

CYPRUS

TSUNAMI
EPICENTER

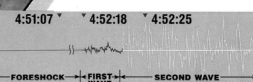

4:51:07 ▼   ▼ **4:52:18**   ▼ **4:52:25**

←———FORESHOCK———→ ←FIRST→ ←———SECOND WAVE———→
                      WAVE

succession of three separate shock waves (above) flattened their hometown of Kourion on July 21, A.D. 365. The final blast leveled structures already weakened by the previous two, thus entombing Kourion's citizens.

The quake also spawned a huge tsunami that devastated eastern Mediterranean coasts; thousands perished in Alexandria, Egypt, 250 miles from the quake's epicenter. The cataclysm preserved a time capsule of daily life reconstructed with careful excavation and electronic technology. One computer-generated map (right) plots finds within a stable where a young girl died, perhaps trying to calm a restless mule. The computer database allows rooms to be analyzed from different angles.

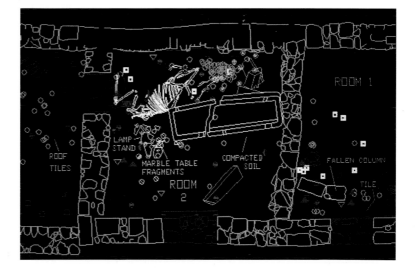

ROOM 1

ROOF
TILES

LAMP
STAND

MARBLE TABLE
FRAGMENTS

COMPACTED
SOIL

FALLEN COLUMN

TILE

ROOM
2

D oll-like remains of a six-month-old Inuit baby (right) survived 500 years of burial in western Greenland, at a long-abandoned Inuit settlement called Qilakitsoq. Dry air and low temperatures preserved his and other bodies through the process of natural mummification, creating a trove of scientific information. Scientists speculate he may have been left exposed to die after his mother's death. He was buried in a common grave with four other people, all interred at different times. X rays of one, a four-year-old boy, revealed a pelvic condition often found in Down's syndrome children. A second grave nearby contained three more bodies, bringing the total to two children and six women whose ages ranged from about 18 to 50.

The bodies were interleaved with skins, and the bottom of each grave was lined with flat stones and grass, all of which contain valuable information about the local people and their environment. Qilakitsoq lay 280 miles north of the Arctic Circle, near a small inlet (above) that opens into Uummannaq fjord. A restored, tight-waisted anorak from the second grave displays stylistic

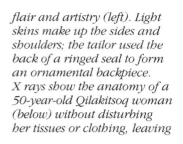

flair and artistry (left). Light
skins make up the sides and
shoulders; the tailor used the
back of a ringed seal to form
an ornamental backpiece.
X rays show the anatomy of a
50-year-old Qilakitsoq woman
(below) without disturbing
her tissues or clothing, leaving

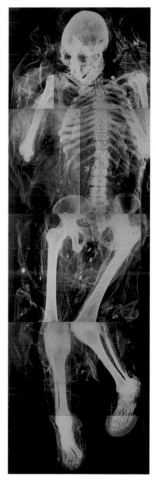

the mummy intact. Infrared
light revealed distinctive
facial tattoos on five of the
women. Identical patterns on
two of them likely indicate
that they were born in the
same community.

amed for the Ötztal
Alps where he was found,
Ötzi the Iceman (right)
constitutes a miracle of
glacial mummification. He
remains one of the oldest and
best-preserved corpses from
prehistoric times. In about
3250 B.C. this solitary traveler
perished of cold and exposure
at 10,530 feet. His corpse lay
under glacial ice for 50
centuries, until mountaineers
discovered the naturally
mummified remains in 1991.
Ötzi lay in a hollow, as if
he had been taking shelter
from a blizzard. His relaxed
limbs suggest he went to

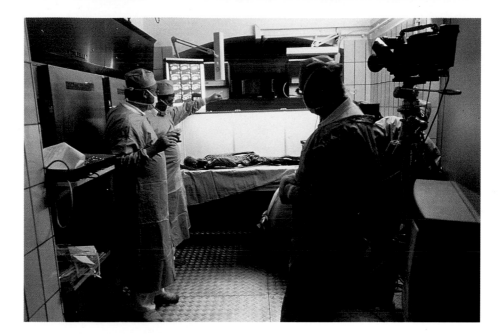

sleep and froze to death.

Today, he lies in a special freezer at the University of Innsbruck (above), where scientists employ the latest archaeological and medical technologies. Using a sterile box, researchers in surgical outfits work on the carefully monitored corpse for only 20 to 30 minutes at a time. Ötzi's possessions tell us he probably climbed into the Alps from the south. He carried high-quality flints that one expert believes were quarried near the Lake Garda region in northern Italy (left). He wore a loincloth and leather

pouch, leggings, a coat, and an outer cape of twisted grass. He carried a backpack, an ax, and a bow. His survival kit included an ash-handled flint dagger and a sheath of twisted grass (above).

Sacrificed five centuries
ago, the 14-year-old Inca girl
known as the Ice Maiden died
on the summit of 20,700-foot
Nevado Ampato, a volcano in
the Peruvian Andes. Anthropologist Johan Reinhard and
his Peruvian assistant Miguel
Zárate (above) found the girl's
mummy bundle, which had
been dislodged from its grave
as the summit ridge collapsed.
Experts at Arequipa's Catholic
University cleared the head of
its cloth wrappings and found
her body (right) even better
preserved than that of Ötzi
the Iceman.

The girl had been wrapped
in a rough outer garment,
then a brown-and-white-
striped cloth. Underneath,
she wore a finely woven dress
and a shawl fastened with a
silver pin (opposite, top). Her
feet bore leather moccasins;
her head, however, was bare.
The artist's depiction includes
a feather headdress similar to
one found later, on another
mummy from Ampato.
Perhaps the Ice Maiden also
wore a headdress originally,
and it was torn off when the

ridge collapsed and her corpse fell from her grave.

Medical technicians at Johns Hopkins Hospital created 3-D video images of her skull (below) by combining 691 computed tomography (CT) scans. Front and side views revealed fractures near her right eye and the cause of death: a massive hemorrhage

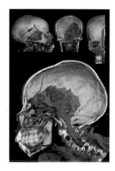

resulting from a swift blow to her head. Blood from the wound had pushed her brain to one side of her skull.

Two thousand years before the ancient Egyptians began mummifying their dead, the Chinchorro culture of Chile and Peru was already hard at work developing its own mummification rites. A young boy's skull, cushioned with a wig of human hair and capped with a black-painted mask of ash paste, joins his body—stuffed with earth and covered with more ash paste—on a reed burial mat (opposite).

By 9000 B.C., the Chinchorro had settled in river valleys that pierce the coast along the Atacama Desert (above), one of the driest environments on earth. Mountain runoff from the distant Andes provided fresh water and vegetation, as well as access to the ocean that sustained small coastal shellfishing camps. Filed down from mussel shells, Chinchorro fishhooks in various stages of completion (below) still litter coastal sites today. Fishing lines consisted of strands of tortora reed intertwined with hair.

rare unlooted tomb in southern Siberia illuminates the culture of ancient Pazyryk herders, who wandered the treeless plains of Russia's Ukok Plateau from the sixth to the second centuries B.C. In 1993, Russian archaeologist Natalya Polosmak excavated the burial chamber (below right), which contained an ice-filled log coffin. Days of drizzling hot water on the coffin (below) eventually revealed the body of a 25-year-old woman wearing an elaborate headdress.

Five feet six inches tall, she had been laid to rest on her side, her strong hands crossed in front of her. The still-soft skin of one shoulder bore an intricate tattoo of a mythical creature (opposite, top left). Her burial robe included a woolen skirt of horizontal white and maroon stripes and a yellow silk top with maroon piping, possibly from China, covering her shoulders. The ice had preserved these and other garments, as well as a wood-backed mirror stashed inside the casket.

Nearby lay the remains of horses (opposite, top right) that had been led to graveside and sacrificed, dispatched with ax blows some 2,400 years ago.

Conservator Marina Moroz looks on as the Pazyryk woman, swathed in gauze

within a plywood hut, awaits transfer to an archaeological laboratory at Novosibirsk.

ANCIENT LANDSC

APES

"An ancient path passes close to the great stone circles, center of an enormous sacred landscape."

I pushed the T-shaped iron rod into the soft bog. One foot…two. The probe sank easily through the dense peat, then struck a subsurface boulder about a yard down. I inserted a bamboo shaft along the iron T, plunging it in until its top was level with that of the rod. Then I withdrew the T and moved one foot to the left. Another push, another hit, this time at only 18 inches depth. Again I placed a bamboo.

Each time, the rod hit rock closer to the surface. A bit farther along it went deeper again. Probe after probe, we traversed ancient fields and the long-forgotten stone walls that delineated them, now mantled in thick peat.

This is archaeology at its traditional best. Without highly technological devices, we use plenty of common sense and the simplest of tools, in this case, a rod used

Phantasmagorical photomontage of Stonehenge highlights the enduring ability of this 5,000-year-old site to fascinate. Both observatory and temple, it was the focal point of a long-lived, largely agrarian society.

by generations of peat cutters to find buried stumps, so as not to damage their prized tools. I am at Céide Fields (pronounced *kay-jeh*, meaning "flat-topped hill") near Ballycastle in Ireland's County Mayo. Here, Stone Age farmers once grazed cattle on rolling, grassy hills and in shallow, fertile river valleys. I am standing on thick peat that covers an entire prehistoric landscape, a hidden checkerboard of stone walls and fields. Half a mile west, forbidding cliffs of limestone tumble 300 feet into the Atlantic Ocean.

"I am my own aborigine," says archaeologist Seamas Caulfield as we gaze out over the undulating bogland. Caulfield had grown up in nearby Belderrig, a hamlet of small houses, where the imprint of history is written with ancient field walls into the land. He remembers as a boy going barefoot for six months of the year, feeling underfoot the texture of the seashore, of pathways, bogs, and small fields.

Caulfield's is the landscape of memory, a tactile relationship between people and the land that sustains them. His father, Patrick, was the local school principal, a man with a passion for the environment and for the past. Like everyone else, he dug peat for fuel in this treeless country. Time and time again, his spade struck buried stone walls. He wrote to Ireland's National Museum, suggesting that the walls were ancient. But no one came to look.

Seamas inherited his father's passion for archaeology and his interest in the stone walls under the peat. As an archaeologist at University College, Dublin, he brought his students to County Mayo, and from 1972 to 1982 they excavated an archaeological site literally at Caulfield's Belderrig doorstep. They uncovered a Stone Age oval enclosure and field walls dating to before 3000 B.C. They also found a Bronze Age round house, walls, and cultivated fields dating to about 1500 B.C.

In 1983 Caulfield began to map the stone walls of Céide Fields, suspecting that they covered many acres. First, he tried using aerial photographs to identify the field systems, but the bog mantled everything. So he turned to the tools of his youth, a six-foot-long iron T-bar and a *slean* (pronounced "shlane"), the spade used to cut peat sods for stacking in piles to dry. Caulfield and his students laid out lines across the hills and ran transects of probes at one-foot intervals across the bogland. Even an untutored novice could become an expert at wall location in a few hours. After a day's work, a line of bamboo canes marked walls and fields.

Archaeologist Gretta Byrne, who now manages the site, holds the record. With a party of three, she probed and mapped six-tenths of a mile of walls in a day. Season after season, Caulfield returned to Céide Fields until he had surveyed more than four square miles of intact farming landscape, one of the largest undisturbed field systems known from the Stone Age.

Céide Fields survives because of unique environmental conditions. With the help of geologists and fossil-pollen experts, Caulfield has reconstructed the dramatic changes in the local landscape over the past 12,000 years. During the Ice Age, Céide Fields was a desolately cold and icy place. After the glaciers retreated, some 11,000 years ago, the climate became warmer and much wetter. Pine forests then covered the rolling hills, forming a landscape quite unlike what appears in the area today. Then the pines suddenly vanished; the perfectly preserved stumps that project through the peat today are the remains of a later forest.

Graduate student Wendy Weiher of Duke University works the rain forest floor in northwestern Belize, matching actual topographic features to the radar image in hand, obtained from high-flying NASA research aircraft. Radar imagery often can lead to finds of previously undetected Maya structures, croplands, and burial sites. It is one more tool in the continuing search for long-vanished landscapes of the ancient world.

Caulfield has taken samples from those stumps and radiocarbon-dated them to about 2800 B.C., anchoring them to a master tree-ring chronology for Ireland that was developed from ancient oak trees. Why did the pine trees vanish so suddenly? Caulfield believes it was the result of local warming, resulting in conditions conducive to grassland rather than forest. Other experts theorize that incoming farmers cleared the trees to graze their cattle. Recent paleobotanical research suggests that the woodland was already opening up prior to settlement.

For nearly 500 years, small groups of farmers and cattle herders settled on the rolling hillsides. As they spread across the undulating land, the newcomers delineated pastures with low stone walls. Their walls tended to be superimposed on the landscape, rather than following the contours of the hillsides, dividing the land into a patchwork of lines, rectangles, and squares. Archaeological maps reveal a buried landscape of at least two parallel field systems, with some of the walls running for more than a mile.

Some limited excavation, undertaken to check the surveys, uncovered stone-ringed pastures remarkably like smaller Irish fields today. Families must have come together to pile boulders into long walls. They divided pastures, then subdivided them again in an ever changing mosaic of fields, modified by successive generations over four or five centuries.

Caulfield has excavated a dwelling, long abandoned amidst the fields. Circular, about 20 feet across, the thatched house stood inside a stone enclosure probably designed to keep stock out of the domestic area. A hearth beside this house has been radiocarbon-dated to a few centuries before 3000 B.C. A few potsherds and stone arrow-heads link the area's long-vanished inhabitants to other farming communities in Ireland and other parts of western Europe at the time.

These farmers lived in small homesteads among their fields. Judging from their communal tombs, they valued their close links to the land. In places, the stone walls give way to megalithic tombs, small burial mounds made up of large stone slabs covered with stone cairns. The slabs form a cruciform sepulchre with a semicircular court outside the entrance.

Generations of the dead lay in the small side chambers. Perhaps the living made offerings to their ancestors in the outside court. Their

gifts ensured the continuity of life and passage of the seasons, which, then as now, governed peoples' lives in this rugged land. Like Seamas Caulfield, the farmers knew every boulder, every tree, every stream. They knew the qualities of grazing grass, used the clouds hugging the cliffs to forecast rain and wind. Theirs was a landscape of folklore too, a spiritual dimension where the ancestors in their tombs guarded the land.

After five centuries, the perennially damp climate defeated the farmers. Wet bog, with its mosses, heathers, and purple moor grass, spread slowly across the hills, mantling the grassland in saturated peat. The cattle herders retreated in the face of the advancing bogland; boundary fences fell into disrepair and were never rebuilt.

Radiocarbon dates from strata immediately above the stone walls tell us the inexorable bog prevailed by about 2400 B.C. But Caulfield is not satisfied with the relatively inaccurate radiocarbon chronology. Fortunately, geologists have found traces of tephra (fine volcanic ash) in the Céide Fields peat, blown all the way from Iceland, some 700 miles to the northwest. Since every Icelandic eruption has produced distinctive and precisely dated tephra deposits, geologists from Queen's University of Belfast believe they will be able to accurately date the Céide strata from tephra samples found there.

No military campaign or social catastrophe disrupted life on the land; the farmers simply moved inland to areas where fertile pastures were abundant. Seamas Caulfield's family has lived at Belderrig for generations. As an archaeologist he can safely claim he is an "aborigine," a distant descendant of the Céide Fields farmers of some 200 generations ago.

During the course of five centuries, the Céide Fields people moved perhaps 250,000 tons of boulders to delineate their fields. Walking over their abandoned pastures, I felt an astounding closeness to them, as if they had left but yesterday, forsaking their houses and their cattle enclosures. This is what makes Céide Fields unique. Most archaeological sites lie among modern settings that bear little resemblance to how they appeared in ancient times.

The best landscape archaeologists rely not only on science and selective excavation, but also on common sense and their own practical experience. One such person was a gentleman antiquarian named John Aubrey. One day in 1649 while hunting, he galloped into the village of Avebury in southern England and found himself surrounded by a deep ditch and mysterious stone circles. He was "wonderfully surprized at the sight of those vast stones: of which I had never heard before" and later returned to sketch and explore. King Charles II learned of Aubrey's descriptions and commanded him to search for human bones.

Aubrey never dug at Avebury, but he made the first survey of what would become recognized as one of Britain's most remarkable sacred

Amateur sleuth searches for remnants of England's Bronze Age at Flag Fen, near Peterborough in central England. Eager to examine large tracts of this landscape, British archaeologist Francis Pryor enlisted the help of a local metal-detector club; its members now "sweep" three different areas of the site each year. One search turned up dozens of bronze artifacts, apparently cast into shallow waters as sacrificial offerings as many as 3,000 years ago.

places. Avebury, he wrote, "did as much excell Stoneheng, as a Cathedral does a Parish church."

Avebury lies on the west side of the Marlborough Downs in north Wiltshire, some 23 miles north of Stonehenge, near the headwaters of the River Kennet. An ancient path passes close to the great stone circles, center of an enormous sacred landscape.

As I wandered between the stone uprights and descended into the ancient ditch, I could almost forget that Avebury had been an integral part of a much larger countryside, which was very different from today's manicured fields and open farmland. You see occasional reminders of that landscape: Barrows—ancient burial mounds—silhouetted against a summer skyline; West Kennet long barrow hugging a ridge; the conspicuous flattened cone of Silbury Hill, a huge and unexplained earthen mound within sight of Avebury. But the pieces are hard to assemble without becoming a bird and taking to the heavens, which is what archaeologists did during and after World War I.

British archaeologist O. G. S. Crawford and many of his colleagues became airmen during the war. They soon realized the potential of aerial photography for recording ancient landscapes. Crawford was a pioneer of nonintrusive archaeology, with a gift for looking at the countryside through archaeological eyes. He had walked over much of Wiltshire, recording earthworks and Roman roads, collecting surface finds from plowed fields, and mapping hundreds of archaeological sites.

Crawford's wartime experience as a navigator caused him to team up with amateur archaeologist and philanthropist Alexander Keiller. Together, they flew hundreds of miles in two months and took some 300 photographs of archaeological sites. *Wessex from the Air,* published in 1928, was the result.

Their aerial views showed Avebury as the major component in a much larger ceremonial landscape made up of causewayed enclosures, long barrows, stone circles, a long avenue, and other structures such as Silbury Hill. Avebury was the focal point of the landscape, with its conspicuous ditch and bank, the stone circles highlighted in oblique light. Some hitherto unknown earthworks showed up as dark soil marks in plowed fields, or as crop marks in ripening ones.

The Avebury landscape evolved over many centuries. By about 4000 B.C. some farmers lived in the region. Three hundred years later, the first burial mounds appeared, and perhaps some simple shrines. As the population increased, people from different kin groups buried their dead in communal graves. The West Kennet long barrow is the most elaborate of excavated shrines in the Avebury area, a sepulchre 330 feet long with five burial chambers and a semicircular forecourt in the center of a facade of upright stones. People buried ancestors in West Kennet for at least three centuries. The site occupied a place on the skyline where, from some angles at least, the presence of these ancestors could be appreciated from afar.

West Kennet went out of use about 2000 B.C., just as construction work on the Avebury stone circles began. When completed, Avebury's outer ditch and bank enclosed 28.5 acres, with a diameter of 1,140 feet. Causewayed entrances divide the enclosed area into four unequal sectors. The flat-bottomed ditch was once between 23 and 30 feet deep and about

40 to 50 feet wide, dug with antler picks and shoulder-blade shovels. Hundreds of people must have labored on the ditch and bank, whose irregular shape testifies to the involvement of different work gangs. There are three stone circles, the outer one originally comprising about a hundred large sandstone blocks known as sarsens, brought from neighboring hills and placed just inside the ditch. Two side-by-side inner circles were aligned more or less north and south. A three-sided arrangement of huge stones once stood in the center of the northern circle; a single upright once marked the center of the southern one.

For all its size and elaboration, the function of Avebury remains a mystery. Clearly, the bank and ditch restricted entry. The earthworks might have provided a grandstand for viewers who witnessed whatever ceremonies unfolded inside. Perhaps only a few people were allowed in the place where initiation rites were performed and ancestors were commemorated. Surrounded by ancestral burial places and by smaller circles, Avebury was the nexus of a vast ceremonial space.

What was this landscape of Stone Age farmland like? No bogland has mantled it, so archaeologists here have used aerial photography and mapping and, more recently, highly selective excavation into earthworks and burial mounds. When the Stone Age builders started construction on a barrow, they buried the original land surface, complete with vegetation and mollusks. Such soils are archaeological microcosms of the ancient land.

Burial mound excavation has changed drastically since Victorian archaeologists sank shafts or dug crude trenches into the centers of barrows in search of burials, cremation urns, or grave furniture. Some diggers, like early 19th-century antiquarian William Cunnington, would open two or three mounds a day. Until about a generation ago, even 20th-century archaeologists believed in total excavation, following the example of Victorian archaeologist Augustus Henry Lane Fox Pitt Rivers, who dissected burial mounds and earthworks on his huge southern England estates with meticulous care in the 1880s and 1890s. Total excavation allowed research teams to reconstruct the entire process of mound building and burial. And it enabled the study of the area's environment on the basis of mollusks and climatic indicators that were preserved on the original burial ground.

Today, however, such large-scale digging is no longer fashionable. Any excavation, no matter how sophisticated, is destruction. So today's fieldworkers rely on small trenches and statistical sampling, knowing that tomorrow's archaeologists may have more refined methods at their disposal. Even a small patch of a site's original ground surface can reveal dramatic climatic change. For example, tiny pollen grains from under the South Street long barrow near Avebury revealed that the area was open tundra at the end of the Ice Age. As global warming continued, temperate forest spread over the land. Then humans cleared the forest, breaking up the newly denuded ground with a simple form of plow now called an ard. The crisscross scratch marks of such plows could be seen in the subsoil during excavation.

Excavators also have found tree holes and shells from mollusks that lived among the roots and tree trunks. More snails found in the turf layer at the bottom of the barrow indicated that the cultivated land had reverted to grassland for a while before the barrow was built, about 3500 B.C.

Almost no undisturbed barrows remain in Wiltshire, and all are protected under law. So in recent years, when archaeologist Alasdair Whittle, of the School of History and Archaeology, University of Wales, Cardiff, wanted to study the ancient environment under Easton Down long barrow southwest of Avebury, he had to request permission to excavate. Permission was granted for only two cuttings, well away from the presumed burial area.

Whittle began with a contour-and-magnetometer survey of the mound, searching for traces of a possible stone-lined burial chamber in the depths of the barrow. The magnetometer measured the remnant magnetism of the soil, searching for anomalies caused by pits, walls, and other features, but found no signs of any.

The two trenches that Whittle dug extended across the ditch that once surrounded the mound. But only one of them cut down to the old land surface and into the very core of the barrow. As the excavators dug down they could see the original tip lines, left as baskets of chalk were piled up on the mound by the builders. The old ground surface yielded mollusk samples, whose shells chronicle dramatic changes in vegetation:

P*atterns of human presence often elude detection on the ground, becoming obvious only from higher up. Aerial photography—which became commonplace during World War I—has proved a most effective survey tool.*

Five concentric stone circles stud the Golan Heights on Israel's northeastern border (right), each ring marking the remains of a rubble wall up to 8 feet high and 11.5 feet wide. This

5,000-year-old Bronze Age structure probably served ceremonial and astronomical functions. A gigantic spider strides Peru's Nazca pampa (left). Puzzling archaeologists and others for generations, the so-called Nazca lines appear to have been integral to a system of sacred landscapes and ceremonies.

Telltale crop mark (right) indicates an otherwise hidden prehistoric enclosure in a field in County Kerry, Ireland.

first woodland, followed by clearance and cultivation, then grassland. When experts Amanda Rouse and John Evans analyzed snail samples from the ditch and from another area of the original land surface, they found a mix of species, both woodland and open-country forms. Perhaps the mound lay near what once had been a boundary between grassland, scrub, and woodland, as if its builders had seen fit to bury their dead near a significant vegetational boundary.

When botanists examined the rather poorly preserved pollen samples from the original turf line, they found that only 4 percent of the pollen came from large tree species, as if the mound had been built in open country. Apparently, it had been a mosaic of grassland, barren ground, bracken, and hazel—precisely what one would expect to find in an area recently cultivated and close to a boundary between grass and woodland.

A sacred and secular landscape lies hidden in the countryside surrounding Avebury. We know of this landscape from isolated snapshots, taken from soils under earthworks and burial mounds, from the ditch of Avebury itself. The countryside once was a jumble of rolling woodland and large clearings where cattle grazed and people raised crops, shifting their small plots regularly, as soils became exhausted.

The great stone circles of Avebury, ancestral burial mounds, and large earthen enclosures lay in the midst of this changing landscape, sometimes set in open country, sometimes in woodland, each with its specific place in a larger whole. Perhaps different rituals took place at various locations, and everything might have been linked by myths and legends that have vanished in the mists of centuries. They survive only in the spatial structuring of the landscape, now revealed by aerial photography, magnetometer survey, and modern environmental science.

Another ancient landscape, this time from the Bronze Age, between 2000 and 1000 B.C., lies at Fengate, just beneath the outskirts of modern Peterborough in central England, and outward into the marshy fens nearby. Archaeologist Francis Pryor spent eight years excavating a network of small fields and drove ways at Fengate, where cattle and brown-fleeced sheep once grazed.

Pryor himself is a sheep farmer. He used his expertise to identify an area of Fengate where Bronze Age farmers had built a stockyard. Here they drove their herds from nearby pastures, herding the animals through a narrow 82-foot-long defile that funneled them into a steady line of easily controlled beasts. The herders used wicker gates to separate the sheep at the end of the race, passing lambs into one enclosure, surplus ewes into another, breeding ewes into a third.

Pryor showed me a 23-foot-long steel race on his own farm, where he dips and sorts his 250-head flock. His modern system looks remarkably similar to the more extensive Bronze Age example, which was big enough to handle a few thousand sheep. From his own farming experience, Pryor knows that the Fengate arrangement would have been effective only with large numbers of animals.

From selective excavation at Fengate, Pryor turned his attention to the wetlands that once lapped this field system. Botanists told him the fens had always been uninhabitable, but Pryor disagreed. For three years he followed his instincts and scoured the banks of modern drainage channels looking for telltale signs of human occupation.

In November 1982, while sketching the layers of an exposed section of Roman road, Pryor stumbled over an oak log in the foggy gloom, the first of many waterlogged planks and timbers that he would uncover within days. His finds extended for more than 260 feet in length under the fen. At first he thought he had found a buried trackway. But when he sank a grid of boreholes in the surrounding fields, Pryor brought up ash and fragments of oak over more than two acres.

Radiocarbon dates placed those timbers at about 1000 B.C. Soon, excavators uncovered wood chips and horizontal timbers resting in a mix of peaty mud and a coarse white sand that must have been brought there from higher ground. Pryor believed these were the remains of a village built on an artificial island in the midst of the fen.

Excavations at Flag Fen have continued ever since and have been in some ways like playing a giant game of pick-up sticks. The diggers uncovered a jumble of planks and smaller timbers, including four rows of posts in irregular lines. Although at first Pryor thought he had found houses on the island, biologist Mark Robinson discovered no traces of the kinds of beetles that feed on damp thatch or decaying organic material found in dwellings. Furthermore, the irregular rows of oak posts extended from the island across to higher ground in both directions.

After more than a decade of research, Pryor now believes the Flag Fen post alignments formed a well-constructed walkway across the watery fen, linking field systems in the surrounding countryside. Tree rings from the posts date the trackway to between 1363 and 967 B.C., a period of nearly 400 years. The labor involved was substantial, perhaps undertaken for more profound reasons than merely ease of communication.

Pryor also has recovered dozens of broken bronze artifacts and human remains from the once waterlogged soil. He believes these were sacrificial offerings from what may have been a symbolic barrier between farmland and the watery world of the fens.

We can imagine the scene. On a cloudy day, the shallow water ripples darkly against the posts. A family walks out, carrying a small bundle of human bones and a bronze sword. They open the bundle and tip the bones into the opaque shallows, smash the blade of the sword and consign it, too, to the water. For a moment, the bright metal flashes before vanishing in the swamp's timeless gloom.

Francis Pryor unraveled the mystery of Flag Fen with a combination of field survey, selective excavation, and highly sophisticated science. But like Céide Fields and Avebury, his patiently exposed landscape may have a profound ritual meaning that still defies our complete understanding.

Many societies used architecture to replicate symbolic landscapes. For example, Palenque, Tikal, and Copan—the great Maya cities of the Mesoamerican lowlands—are depictions in stone, earth, and plaster of the ancient Maya world. Their temple-pyramids represent sacred mountains; temple entrances signify doorways leading to the underworld; and carved stelae, set in open plazas, are the trees of a symbolic forest.

Generations of archaeologists have studied the architecture of plaza and pyramid, a task made easier by the decipherment of Maya glyphs. We now have a basic understanding of the Maya cosmos and the architecture that reflected it. In recent years archaeologists have moved out into the surrounding countryside to answer new questions. How did the Maya feed themselves and support imposing cities? And above all, why did Maya civilization suddenly collapse in the southern lowlands about A.D. 900?

Maya archaeologists have offered many explanations for the collapse: Chronic warfare; excessive demands on commoners by authoritarian leaders, which led to a breakdown of political authority; huge population growth; and ecological collapse, which resulted from overexploitation of the environment. Some of these factors must have left lasting impressions on the landscape in the form of changing settlement distributions and population shifts. A remarkable, long-term campaign of nonintrusive archaeology in the hinterland of Copan, Honduras, provides new insights into the possible causes of the collapse.

Copan's core covers an area of some 36 acres, rising from the vast open spaces of the Great and Middle Plazas to an elaborate complex of raised and enclosed courtyards and temple-pyramids. Maya archaeologist Sylvanus G. Morley was so impressed by the city that he called it the "Athens of the New World." Here Maya architecture and sculpture achieved their greatest distinction, as ruler after ruler built his architectural statement atop those of his predecessors.

A combination of archaeology and deciphered glyphs has given us an outline of Copan's long history. The earliest inscription dates to 11 December A.D. 435, when Kinich Yax Kuk Mo ("Sun-eyed Green Quetzal Macaw") founded a dynasty that ruled for four centuries. Copan soon became a major kingdom of the Maya world. By the eighth century, more than 10,000 people lived in the Copan Valley close to the capital.

For nearly 25 years, American and Honduran archaeologists have cooperated on an ambitious long-term research project at Copan. Within the city itself, a team of archaeologists and epigraphers led by William L. Fash, now of Harvard University, have reconstructed an elaborate Hieroglyphic Stairway leading to Temple 26, which was dedicated around A.D. 750 by the ruler Smoke Shell. His son Yax Pasah ("First Dawn") was the last lord of Copan, ruling in troubled times.

By then, the self-perpetuating Maya nobility had grown to almost unmanageable size, with every member expecting the privileges of the elite. Copan society had become top-heavy and riddled with factionalism. Not even the ruler's prestige could ward off Copan's collapse by the end of the ninth century. The question is whether this collapse had been mirrored in changing population distributions.

From 1960 to 1975, Pennsylvania State University archaeologists led by William T. Sanders surveyed the Basin of Mexico, recording every site they could find. This classic instance of nonintrusive archaeology showed how human settlement changed dramatically with the rise of the city of Teotihuacan in the first millennium A.D. A thousand years later, the settlement distribution shifted again. More than 250,000 people lived close to the Aztec capital, Tenochtitlan, in A.D. 1500.

In the mid-1970s, Gordon R. Willey began a multidisciplinary approach for mapping and excavating in the Copan Valley. Willey and his students reconstructed the ancient settlement patterns near Copan through site survey, transit mapping, and excavation.

In the 1980s, researchers headed by Sanders and David Webster revised and expanded Willey's approach to survey the hinterland of the city of Copan. Successive research teams have located and mapped more than 52 square miles around the urban core, focusing on the areas most suitable for human settlement. Aerial photographs and foot surveys have recorded 1,425 archaeological sites in the Copan Valley, containing more than 4,500 structures.

The researchers mapped and surface-collected each site. They developed a hierarchy of different site types, from complex villages to isolated hamlets and dwellings, as a way of studying changing patterns of settlement. The survey revealed an urban core, a densely occupied area surrounding the city, and a rural region with a much lower population density.

Surface survey, combined with the collection of artifacts, revealed the major parameters of human settlement but gave only a general impression of changes in population distribution over the centuries. The researchers had systematically selected a sample of 252 archaeological sites throughout the valley and had test-excavated most of them, digging hundreds of small pits. The lack of change in pottery styles, combined with the limited number of radiocarbon samples, proved insufficient to link the sites to the master chronological sequence at Copan that had been developed from stratified trenches in the core city.

The excavations, however, had yielded an abundance of artifacts fashioned from obsidian, in both the central core and in outlying rural settlements. Obsidian, basically natural glass formed by volcanic activity, was highly prized and traded all over Mesoamerica.

To archaeologists, obsidian's importance stems from not only its beauty but also its datability. A freshly worked surface of obsidian absorbs a small but measurable amount of water from its surroundings, forming a hydration layer invisible to the naked eye. This layer contains about 3.5 percent water, which increases its density and allows it to be measured accurately under polarized light. The depth of the hydration layer represents the time since the object was manufactured or used, although much depends on local environmental variables such as temperature.

Since the Copan Obsidian Hydration Dating Project began in 1984, it has yielded some 2,300 dates from the 252 sites, more than 14 percent of all known sites in the entire Copan Valley. The method used—obsidian hydration measurement—proved ideal for Copan, where radiocarbon and archaeomagnetic dates are rare and expensive. Obsidian hydration is relatively cheap.

Archaeologist AnnCorinne Freter and her colleagues took great pains to develop background environmental data. They buried thermal cells at various depths in the sites to be dated. They also collected soil composition measurements over multiyear periods. At the same time, a comprehensive sampling strategy ensured that dates came from a variety of obsidian objects, covering the entire span of the deposits. Copan's obsidian came from several easily identifiable sources, so the researchers could use the distinctive chemical characterizations from dated artifacts to deduce changes in obsidian trade through time. Thus, the researchers checked the accuracy of obsidian hydration dates at every turn.

The Copan surveys chronicle the remarkable demographic changes that unfolded around the city during the course of four centuries. They show how, between A.D. 550 and 700, the Copan state expanded rapidly, with most of the population concentrated in the urban core and immediate peripheral zones; its rural population remained small and scattered. From A.D. 700 to 850, the Copan Valley saw a rapid population increase to between 20,000 and 25,000 people.

These figures, calculated from site size, suggest that the local population was doubling every 80 to 100 years, with about 80 percent of the people living within the city core and its immediate periphery. Rural settlement had expanded outward along the valley floor, but was remaining relatively scattered. People had begun to farm less fertile foothill areas, however, as the population density of the urban core increased. One indication of the extreme stratification of Copan society is that 82 percent of the population lived in humble dwellings.

The ruling dynasty ended in 820. Forty years later, rapid depopulation began. The urban core and periphery zones lost about half their people after 850, while the rural population increased by almost 20 percent. Small regional settlements replaced the scattered villages of earlier times, a response to cumulative deforestation, overexploitation of marginal agricultural soils, and sheet erosion near the capital.

By 1150, the Copan Valley population had fallen to between 5,000 and 8,000. Today's archaeologists, drawing on years of remote sensing, field survey, and test excavations, have documented that massive shifts in farming settlements occurred around the city. The evidence hints that environmental degradation was a major factor in the Maya collapse.

Archaeologists have also moved into space. For example, they send instruments into orbit on space shuttles to document the impact of humanity on the world's environments. In addition, they use imagery from satellites to obtain unexpected information on ancient societies.

The Great Wall of China is visible with the naked eye from a space shuttle. On radar images, it appears as a thin orange band. The latest generation of radar operates in different frequencies and wavelengths, allowing the scanner to "see" through sand, ice, and vegetation, under certain conditions. Two wavelengths are now polarized, so the signals can be received and transmitted both vertically and horizontally. As a result, scientists have detected from space two generations of the Great Wall: the original, now partially buried Sui Dynasty wall of 1,500 years ago and the Ming Dynasty wall of 600 years ago.

In 1981 the space shuttle *Columbia*, as part of a geology mission to look at the surface of the earth, directed its imaging radar system at the world's major deserts. The images identified ancient riverbeds buried in bedrock 10 to 16 feet below the surface of the Sahara. When geologists and archaeologists field-checked the sites, they found 200,000-year-old stone axes in the long-buried river deposits. Archaeologists had long believed the now-arid Sahara had once been a vital highway for early humans moving from the tropics into more temperate latitudes. Radar imagery provided dramatic proof that their theories were correct.

The Arabian Peninsula's Rub al Khali, the Empty Quarter, is one of the most inhospitable regions on earth. Few archaeologists had ventured into its wastes until NASA scientists at the Jet Propulsion Laboratory used radar imagery from space to delineate hitherto invisible desert tracks across the arid landscape. The tracks converged on the long-vanished site of Shisur in Oman, a major center of the frankincense trade from 1000 B.C. to A.D. 400, and possibly the mythical "lost city" of Ubar.

In Cambodia, also, the great reservoirs surrounding the temple complex of Angkor show up clearly in the new radar imagery. The Khmer civilization of Angkor reached the height of its prosperity between A.D. 900 and 1200. Each Khmer king surrounded himself with artists, poets, and sculptors, whose sole tasks were to embellish and adorn their magnificent capitals. In the 12th century, King Suryavarman II built Angkor Wat, the largest religious building in the world.

Angkor Wat, rising in three great squares, dwarfs even the Pyramids of Giza by the Nile. Every detail of this extraordinary building reproduces part of the heavenly world in a terrestrial mode. The Khmer believed the world consisted of a central continent, known as Jambudvipa, with the cosmic mountain Meru rising from its center. Their Hindu gods lived at the summit of Meru, represented at Angkor by the highest tower. The remaining four central towers depict Meru's lesser peaks; the enclosure wall, the mountain range at the edge of the world; and the surrounding moat, the ocean beyond. Angkor Wat was a monument to Vishnu, the preserver. Facing west, the direction of death, it also served both as a state temple for the king during his lifetime and a mausoleum upon his death.

In 1994, the shuttle *Endeavour* flew over Angkor in an intentional routing to locate archaeological sites hidden in the dense Cambodian forest. Elizabeth Moore, at the School of Oriental and African Studies, University of London, has identified more than ten mound sites, some with vestiges of encircling moats and earthworks. The majority of sites are inaccessible, but their form suggests they predate the classic era.

The temple complex of Angkor Wat shows up as a rectangle surrounded by a 650-foot-wide dark border: the city moat. A network of ancient and modern roads appears on the satellite images. The data from the imaging radar will help map the vast system of canals, reservoirs, and other works built during the city's heyday. Remote sensing from space may also help establish why the site was abandoned in the 15th century.

Radar imagery from space and other remote-sensing technologies represent the high point of nonintrusive archaeology. They are at their best when combined with other remote-sensing data acquired from aerial photographs and ground-penetrating radar. Most remote-sensing methods rely on measuring the physical properties of the soil and anything else on the surface. Optical satellite imagery and aerial photographs measure reflections of light within the visible spectrum; radar images do the same for the microwave portion of the electromagnetic spectrum, not visible to the human eye.

Few archaeologists have combined all these approaches into an integrated view of ancient landscapes, using Geographic Information Systems (GIS) technology. GIS

The infrared eye reveals all—almost. Pre-Columbian canals, long silted over, show up as faint lines in this infrared aerial photograph taken near Santa Luisa, in Veracruz, Mexico. Combining such technology with ground surveys enabled archaeologists to map a Maya irrigation system here that once produced abundant maize, beans, and other crops, some of which probably was sent as tribute to overlords in the city of El Tajin.

comprise complex computer programs that can handle spatial data, such as maps, as well as text and number data. This means the researcher can digitize a series of maps into a computer, stacking information—archaeological sites and features, rock types, soils, topographic variations, vegetation, and such—as individual maps on top of one another.

The data come from many sources: aerial photographs, field surveys, radar images, and various subsurface detection systems such as magnetometers or ground-penetrating radar. Scientists can even produce computer-generated maps and simulations as models to superimpose on conventional maps. Once stored in GIS, data can be displayed as vector maps, like those used for automobile travel, which have lines that represent rivers, roads, and land-use areas. The system also can generate raster maps, which divide a region into rows and columns of "cells," each cell representing a segment of specific landscape information. GIS databases take time to develop, but offer almost open-ended potential for answering questions about ancient landscapes. The Wroxeter Hinterland Project, for example, has broken new ground with its innovative use of GIS to survey the relationship between a Roman town and its surroundings.

Viroconium Cornoviorum, the Roman town at present-day Wroxeter, near Shrewsbury in west-central England, was the fourth largest urban area in Roman Britain. Wroxeter began as a legionary fortress in A.D. 60, then became a town in its own right 30 years later, flourishing until the fifth or sixth century. Unlike Roman London or York, much of Wroxeter now lies under pastureland rather than under city concrete. As such, it is accessible for archaeological survey, and archaeologists have studied the major public buildings and commercial zones of the town for more than a century, excavating no more than 5 percent of its surface.

Since World War II, researchers have used aerial photographs to map the general layout of the settlement and have used potsherds and other artifacts to develop a detailed chronology. But aerial photography and excavation together could not answer many fundamental questions about the history of one of Roman Britain's most important towns.

Wroxeter was a strategic military gateway into neighboring Wales; many camps and forts lay close to the town. What impact did these army encampments have on the rural population? What were the consequences

Desolate sea of dunes, the Rub al Khali, or Empty Quarter, blankets some 250,000 square miles of the Arabian Peninsula. Ridges of windblown sand show yellow in this false-color Landsat image; blue areas represent limestone basins. Radar-based imagery helped NASA scientists Ron Blom and Robert Crippen identify virtually invisible 1,500- to 2,000-year-old tracks that once led to the frankincense-rich site of Shisur, possibly the "lost city" of Ubar.

of Roman conquest on the indigenous Iron Age farmers? Wroxeter's researchers suspected that the settlement pattern of the hinterland was much more complex than often assumed.

A new generation of archaeologists, among them Vince Gaffney of the University of Birmingham, realized that GIS, when combined with remote sensing and traditional ground survey, had the potential to answer these and many other questions.

Fortunately, archaeologists could draw on a massive archive of aerial photographs of the surrounding landscape, taken under all weather conditions over more than a half century. Hundreds of crop marks appear in these images, most of them being farming enclosures and the remains of once extensive field systems. About 400 such enclosures have come to light in the Wroxeter hinterland alone. But only about 5 percent of them have been excavated or surveyed, leaving many questions unanswered.

The research teams worked with images from exceptionally dry summers like 1976, when Roman walls (marked by dead grass) showed up clearly on aerial photographs. Another good year was 1996, when the researchers were able to check crop marks on the ground that had showed up from the air. They "warped" digital images of the photographs onto the national map grid, tying them as closely as possible to specific locations. The images became actual maps, which were on a known scale. Now fieldworkers could measure and interpret such features as the Roman street grid with margins of error as small as three feet.

The Wroxeter Hinterland Project relies heavily on volunteer fieldworkers, from teenagers to senior citizens, who spend days and weeks acquiring survey information to improve the accuracy of the town and hinterland maps. One group is recording the Roman town's topography, taking measurements every 10 meters (nearly 33 feet). Their highly accurate data enable the researchers to map archaeological features in aerial photographs with even greater accuracy.

A magnetometer survey of Wroxeter is also under way, producing new data on the street plan. This survey is revealing hitherto unknown buildings, including rows of shops and temples. For years, experts had pointed to the gaps in the street plan and called Wroxeter a garden city, replete with numerous parks, trees, and open spaces. The magnetometers, however, have proved them wrong. They detected some anomalies on the north side of town, where the regular street plan gives way to more irregular settlement. Such areas indicate growth by natural expansion rather than by the careful planning so typical of Roman authorities.

Wroxeter's researchers are also trying ground-penetrating radar, which aims high-frequency waves (similar to those used in domestic microwave ovens) into the ground. The waves bounce off buried walls and other features. When run along parallel lines, this system produces profiles of subsurface features and records them into a computer. The resulting "slices" of the soil are then processed digitally, to fill in gaps in the data and to enhance often barely detectable structures. Radar profiles may add additional precision to the town map.

The Wroxeter project is unique, because GIS allows the researcher to manipulate on the computer screen all available archaeological data that has been digitized, to generate all kinds of highly accurate maps of town and hinterland—this with minimal excavation. On-the-ground surveys and

GIS form a powerful tool for studying ever changing ancient landscapes. For example, Wroxeter's archaeologists can answer questions about changing patterns of supply-and-demand by assuming the town was the economic center of the surrounding region in Roman times. Their data, based on remote sensing and actual artifacts recovered from specific sites, allow them to show how mass-produced pottery flowed through the region along an existing infrastructure of roads, tracks, and rivers.

They can show which villages and farmsteads would have had the best and worst access to the merchandise and then compare GIS data with the actual potsherds found during field walking and excavation. The team can examine much more abstruse relationships, as well. How do different pottery types vary with different field systems? Were there connections between social ranking and different segments of the economy?

At Céide Fields I traversed a landscape that had been revealed with the simplest of field techniques. At Wroxeter I explored a long-vanished landscape with the help of the infinitely manipulable data-crunching machine, the computer.

As I probed a three-dimensional image of the Roman town—the virtual Wroxeter—I pondered the future: almost no excavation? Instead, virtual reality, leading you by the hand through a digitally reconstructed town? An ability to look at ancient societies in hitherto unimaginable ways?

Time and time again, I have stood on a puzzling archaeological site and wished I could voyage freely underground without the tyranny and labor of excavation. Perhaps those days lie in the not-too-distant future.

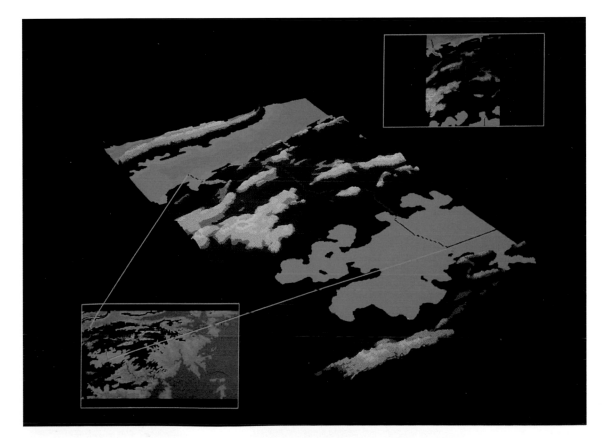

Built as a communal tomb in about 2500 B.C., Poulnabrone dolmen—its name means

"hole of the sorrows"—stands against the late afternoon sky over Ireland's County Clare.

igsaw puzzle of ancient timbers fascinates archaeologists of all ages at England's Flag Fen, where thousands of jumbled, 3,000-year-old logs compose a 3.5-acre platform (below). Working under an all-weather shelter, Francis Pryor supervises the raising of delicate timbers (left) only after the positions of every plank and upright have been recorded. To avoid sinking into the peat-like deposits, excavators squat on kneelers and boards. Perfectly preserved by the wet fen, more than 30,000 oak planks, logs,

and other wood fragments have been mapped and carefully examined for traces of cut marks, which can yield valuable information on the age and type of ax used.

Trying to decipher the tangled remains, wood expert Maisie Taylor and student Martin Redding pore over a transparent map of the main dig at Flag Fen (right). After a decade of excavation, mystery still surrounds the platform, joined to neighboring high ground by a rough post causeway. The fen's Bronze Age residents threw valuable

metal items such as swords and bronze shears (below) into the dark, shallow water, apparently as ritual offerings.

Such objects came from as far away as the Alps; the wealth needed to acquire them was produced by the farmers, whose large flocks of sheep were kept in neat fields and paddocks around the fen's edges. A classic example of modern archaeology carried out with painstaking thoroughness, Flag Fen was probably a sacred landscape that marked the boundary between the living and spiritual worlds. Deciphering its maze of timbers will continue for decades to come.

tone model of the Hindu universe, Angkor Wat (right) stands majestic on the fertile plain between Cambodia's Kulen Hills and the lake of Tonle Sap. Its five central towers depict peaks of Mount Meru, mythical center of the Hindu realm. Between the 9th and 13th centuries A.D., Khmer kings built successive capitals here, raising temples to glorify their lives and ensure their immortality.

King Suryavarman II began Angkor Wat around 1113, dedicating it to the Hindu god Vishnu and financing it with spoils of war. It remains the grandest and most venerated of the region's 72 major monuments. Myriad artisans, workers, and slaves took 37 years to complete this masterpiece. Its outer gallery, half a mile in circumference, contains continuous bas-reliefs that recount myths of the gods, display scenes of graceful dancers, and depict the Khmer army in full array.

Radar images such as one taken from the space shuttle Endeavour in 1994 (below) reveal a wealth of ancient sites surrounding the main temple. Also visible are large rectangular reservoirs, linked by a complex system of moats, canals, and dikes into a sophisticated hydraulic system used to meet the needs of agriculture, transportation, and religion.

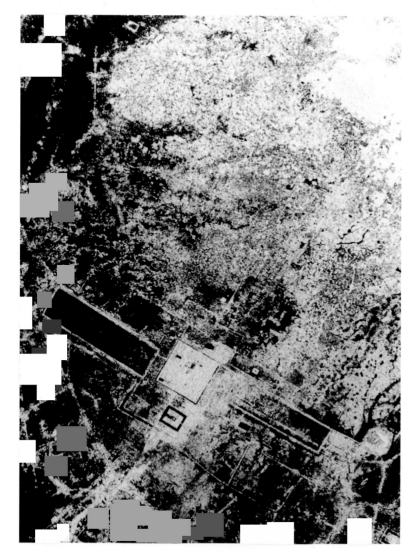

G *hostly reconstruction of the long-vanished Temple of Amun (right) hovers anew over the shrine's surviving lower walls near Jebel Barkal, Sudan, once site of the capital of the Kingdom of Kush. Thus do today's architectural computer programs help archaeologists revisit ancient landscapes. Members of an expedition from Boston's*

Museum of Fine Arts, led by archaeologist Timothy Kendall, first measured the temple's courtyard, now buried in sand (upper left). From this they developed a "wire-frame" computer model of the complete structure (lower left). Another program translated those dimensions into realistic images that

could be "ghosted" over the site photograph.

Jebel Barkal, a sandstone butte 20 miles downstream from the Fourth Cataract of the Nile, once marked the southern limit of Egyptian empire. It was considered the chief southern residence of the god Amun; pharaohs from Thutmose III to Ramses II (about 1460 to 1250 B.C.) built an elaborate religious complex here to mirror grand Karnak, at Thebes. Kings of Kush, converts to the worship of Amun, restored this sanctuary by about 750 B.C. and continued to maintain it until the fourth century A.D., after which it fell into ruin and was buried by sand.

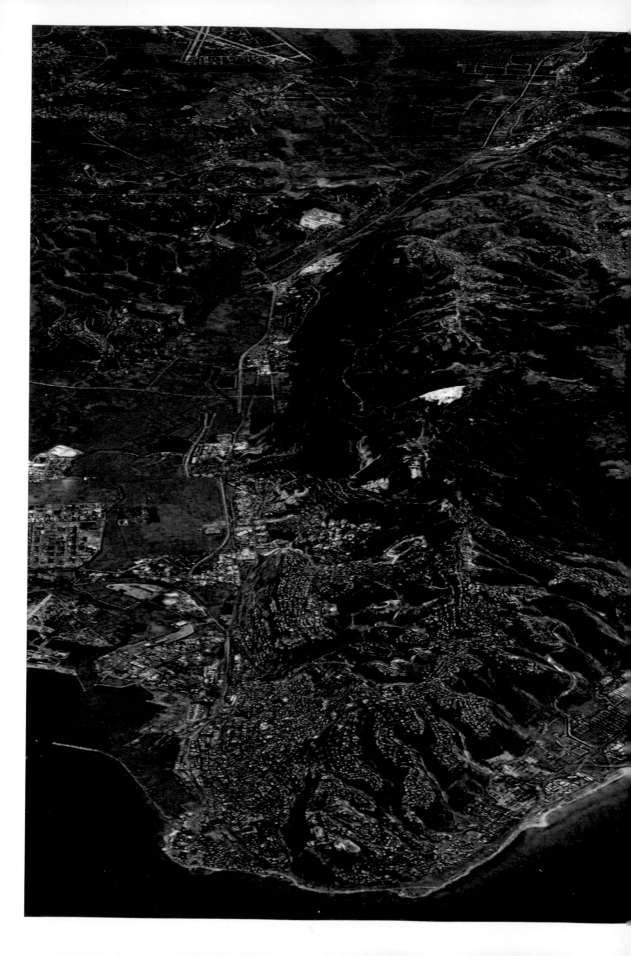

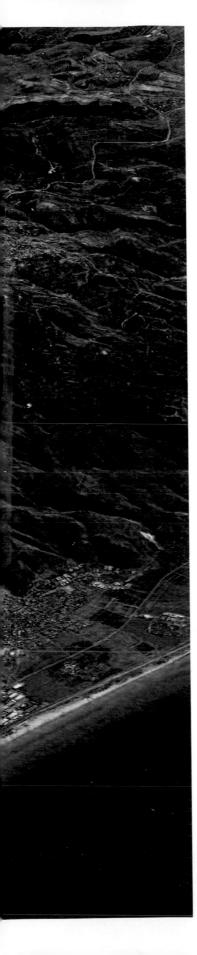

ot an aerial photo but a computer simulation, this oblique view of the Israeli city of Haifa (left) captures the three-dimensional feel of a flyover. It all began with a very flat but high-resolution image, produced after the Landsat 5 satellite passed 440 miles above the Holy Land on a cloudless day in 1987. Technicians at Earth Satellite Corporation in Rockville, Maryland, later enhanced the natural color resolution with much finer gray-scale detail from a French SPOT satellite, producing an even more detailed overview of the area (right, top).

Next, John K. Hall of the Geological Survey of Israel made a digital terrain model from detailed topographic maps. That model, which consists of elevations distributed on a 25-meter grid, can be used to present topographic information as a color-coded contour map (right, middle), or as a mesh-relief model (right, bottom). At the Technion—the Israel Institute of Technology—computers merged the satellite data with the elevation data, in effect "draping" the satellite image over the relief map. Specially designed software enabled project coordinator Richard Cleave to produce the final, three-dimensional version.

So it is that archaeologists now can effectively "fly" over a key site, viewing it from any angle or height—without leaving the ground. They also can exaggerate relief to emphasize detail, model ancient environmental alterations through a few keystrokes, and perhaps gain new insights into many archaeological landscapes.

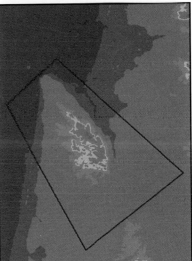

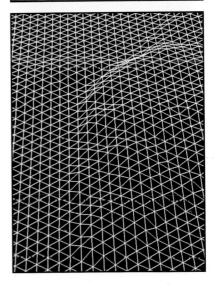

Mountains man-made and natural converge at Teotihuacan, Mesoamerica's first

metropolis, where the Pyramid of the Sun looms more than 200 feet skyward.

onument to Maya genius, the metropolis of El Mirador (right) was home to tens of thousands during its brief Preclassic-period heyday, from 150 B.C. to A.D. 150. Later abandoned, its many temple-pyramids and plazas were soon reclaimed by tropical forest. Similar fate befell ruins at Nakbe, nearly eight miles away (opposite, in foreground, with El Mirador on the horizon).

Remote-sensing specialist Daniel Lee processed data

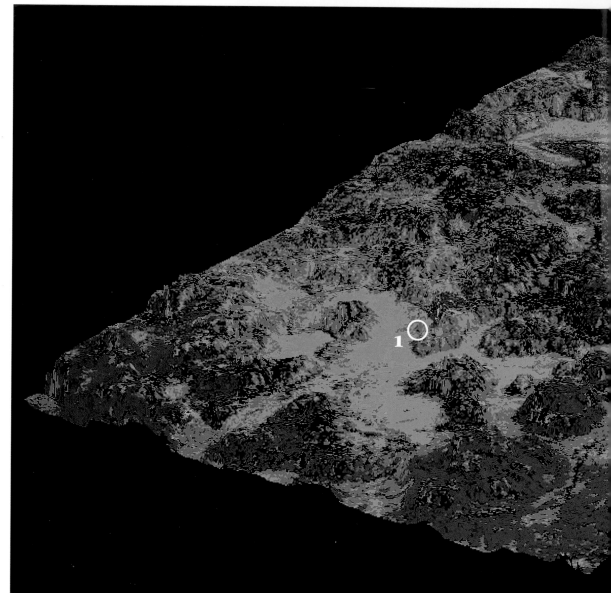

from the Landsat 5 satellite to produce a topographic map of the El Mirador region (below). Rendering the information in perspective, he exaggerated heights by 20 percent for emphasis; different plants account for the various red and green hues. Maya builders had located both El Mirador (1) and Nakbe (2) on relatively high ground alongside seasonal swamps (blue) that served as important sources of water. Probable trade routes between

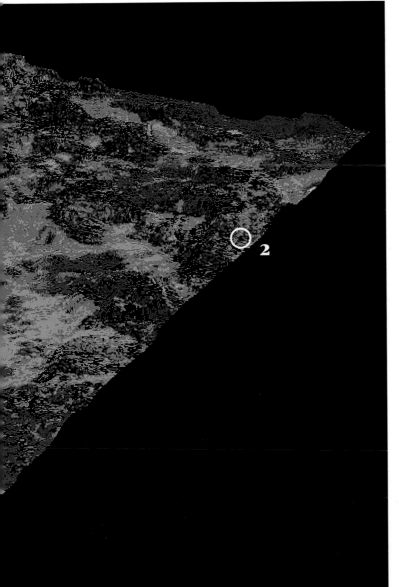

these and other ancient cities also can be reconstructed by manipulating digital data.

Now covered with dense vegetation, such sites gleamed bright in the tropical sun of 2,000 years ago, surrounded by intricate patchworks of cleared fields, swamp gardens, and outlying settlements. Excavations at El Mirador by Ray T. Matheny, of Brigham Young University, revealed a remarkably well-preserved city, one that was never torn down or substantially remodeled by Classic Maya people. At its height it covered some six square miles, with its Tigre Pyramid and Danta Complexes towering over the surrounding landscape.

Remnant of artificial islands originally farmed by the Aztec, the last of Tenochtitlan's fertile

chinampas—*floating gardens—today endure within a park at Xochimilco, Mexico City.*

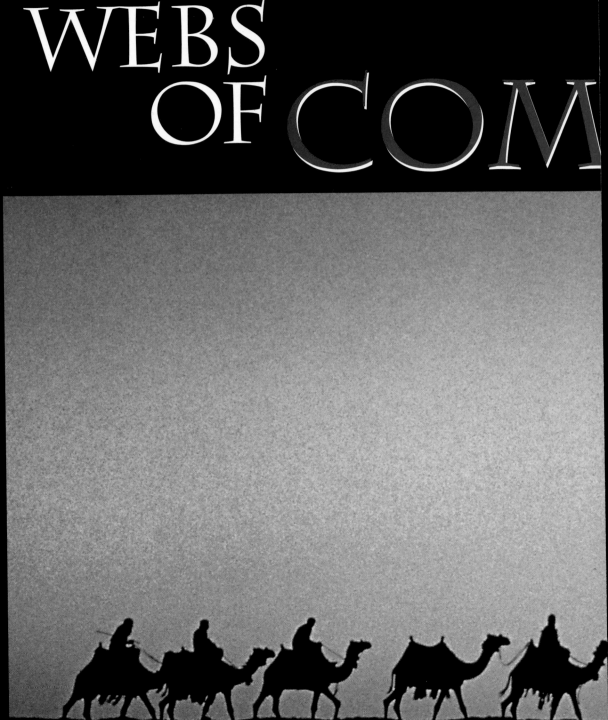

WEBS
OF COM

MERCE

We found the collapsed walls of the small hut five feet down amid Isamu Pati, a thousand-year-old farming village high on Zambia's Batoka Plateau. Piece by piece we lifted fire-hardened wall fragments, gradually exposing a hearth and old grinding stones on the floor beneath. As I scraped and brushed around the circular foundation, I came across the telltale softness of a grave, marked with a solitary stone.

I spent hours on my hands and knees with brush and dental pick, exposing from the head downward the skeleton of a young male crouched in a shallow burial pit. Suddenly my soft brush displaced a small red glass bead, just below the chin. I teased fine gray soil from three more beads lying in a short string around the man's neck. Red glass beads were the last thing I had expected

to find 600 miles from the Indian Ocean. African artisans never made glass beads, so someone had to have carried strings of Indian beads deep into the African interior. Months, perhaps years, later, a few of them found their way from village to village and finally to this remote Batoka Plateau settlement far from any mineral deposits or strategic trade routes.

Perhaps I should not have been surprised, for some months later I met an old African man, who in his youth had walked all the way from his Zambian home to the banks of the Zambezi River in Mozambique, a distance of at least 400 miles. Such journeys once were commonplace, he told me, along narrow intervillage paths.

Arab glass, glass beads, coins, Chinese porcelain, Indian Ocean seashells: Archaeologists measure the tentacles of Indian Ocean trade in Africa's interior by exotic objects found in their excavations. Objects that must have been common on the coast probably assumed enormous prestige and value in the interior. In 1854 the Scottish missionary and explorer David Livingstone visited Chief Shinte of the Balonda tribe in western Zambia. As Livingstone was about to leave, the chief gave him a necklace made of beads and the conical end of a single *Conus* shell from the Indian Ocean. The going price for such shells was two for a slave, five for a tusk of elephant ivory. Three-quarters of a century later, *Conus* shells still commanded high prices in the far interior. Enterprising European traders even sold porcelain replicas of the shells to African villagers.

Isolated artifacts like glass beads provide hardly more information than a dot on a distribution map, perhaps a link in a trade route that once brought such beads up the Zambezi Valley, or other routes that conveyed Baltic amber to Italy or obsidian mirrors from Mexico's Gulf lowlands to its central valley. Since all trade depends on the laws of supply and demand, an insatiable desire in distant India for gold and soft, easily carved African elephant ivory brought traders to the Mozambique coast and the Zambezi River. They carried rolls of cheap cloth and strings of beads upstream, exchanging them for many times their worth in gold, ivory, and other raw materials.

Until just before Portuguese explorer Vasco da Gama arrived on the Mozambique coast in 1497, a group of African traders lived on a low hill named Ingombe Ilede ("the place where the cow lies down") in the middle Zambezi Valley. Ingombe Ilede is far from any gold or copper outcrops, yet four people found buried atop the hill wore necklaces of gold beads and finely made copper-wire bangles on their arms. The Ingombe Ilede people manufactured their own copper bangles; tongs, wire-drawing tools, and trade wire also were found with the four skeletons. Copper salts in the bangles had preserved several layers of cotton fabric and bark cloth, remnants of long cotton robes and bark-cloth shrouds. Heavy necklaces of imported glass beads in many colors also adorned the dead. One of them had a necklace of nine *Conus* shells.

Other exotic artifacts here originated as far afield as India, the East African coast, the Zambian copper belt, and northern Zimbabwe. David Livingstone noted the region's fame for its salt deposits—a vital commodity to stock-raising farmers, both in his day and in earlier times. Perhaps the Ingombe Ilede people benefited from their strategic position by the Zambezi, trading gold, copper, and ivory for cloth, glass beads, and seashells, and then using them to acquire minerals from many miles away.

Long considered the queen of textiles, silk has attracted consumers and traders for centuries. This sumptuous, silk-embroidered coat and waistcoat from France mark an apogee of 18th-century fashion. Silk remained China's secret for more than 2,000 years. Early in the second century B.C., caravans began to link East and West, bringing silk, jade, and spices to the Mediterranean world. The Romans valued silk as highly as gold, but—according to legend—did not acquire silkworms themselves until the sixth century A.D.

*ewards of
empire glisten in
bas-relief along the
eastern staircase of
the Apadana, royal
audience hall of
ancient Persepolis.
This particular section
depicts tribute-bearing
Gandarians and
Bactrians offering the
Persian king lances
and a humped bull,
vessels and a Bactrian
camel. Cypress trees
separate different
delegations, each led
by a hand-clasping
Mede or Persian.
Together, the groups
represent the 23
lands ruled by Darius
and Xerxes.*

*Whether in tribute or
in outright trade, such
accounts of exchanges
provide archaeologists
with invaluable
insights, helping them
chronicle the webs of
commerce and empire
that once held sway.*

Historically, finding such trade goods told us next to nothing about the ebb and flow of ideas, about the precise sources of raw materials, or about the men and women engaged in ancient trade on land and sea. When James Chaplin and I excavated Ingombe Ilede in the early 1960s—before archaeologists regularly used high-tech methods to identify the sources of raw materials—we could only speculate about the sources of the copper and gold in the village. Just a generation later, sourcing or "characterization" studies that use spectrographic analysis have become routine.

Today, modern spectrometric methods rely on the physical properties of atoms to identify and calculate trace elements. They use a variety of methods to excite atoms and detect the resulting release of energy. The process produces an analysis of an artifact, usually without destroying it, an important consideration with fragile and unique objects.

Obsidian is fine-grained volcanic glass, much prized by prehistoric toolmakers (and even some contemporary ones). Modern-day lithic technologists often use it to replicate ancient stone artifacts of all kinds, employing techniques identical to those used by the ancients. Controlled experiments by archaeologist J. Jeffrey Flenniken and others have shown how Paleo-Indians of 10,000 years ago thinned the bases of their stone projectile points. Even today some surgery is performed with razor-sharp obsidian blades. Obsidian is the ultimate toolmaking stone, a rare commodity found at precious few locations. Fortunately, obsidian from each source has a slightly different chemical composition due to trace elements. Using techniques of mass spectrometry, an expert can pinpoint the exact origin of even a small fragment.

Precise sourcing has proved to be a powerful technique for studying ancient trade. In the seventh millennium B.C., for example, farmers in

Cyprus, in Turkey, and in the Jordan Valley obtained obsidian from two sources in central Turkey; villagers in the Zagros Mountains and other parts of southern Iran obtained their obsidian from eastern Turkey. Cambridge University archaeologist Colin Renfrew, a pioneer in sourcing research, plotted the percentage of obsidian in each village on a logarithmic scale against distance. He found that the proportion of obsidian fell off exponentially, the farther a site was from the source. Renfrew believes this ancient trade was a classic example of down-the-line bartering, as lumps of valuable obsidian passed from village to village. Ancient Greeks also collected volcanic glass from the Cycladic island of Melos as early as 8000 B.C.—the earliest known evidence for Mediterranean seafaring. On the other side of the world, oceangoing canoes carried obsidian from the Bismarck Archipelago region of the western Pacific eastward to Vanuatu, a distance of more than 1,500 miles, over 3,000 years ago.

Sourcing came into its own when a 3,300-year-old tragedy provided experts from the Institute of Nautical Archaeology (INA) at Texas A&M

University with a unique portrait of maritime trade in the eastern Mediterranean during the Late Bronze Age. In 1982 sponge diver Mehmet Çakir spotted what he called "metal biscuits with ears" on the seafloor off Uluburun, a headland in southern Turkey. His skipper knew at once what he had found, and reported the find to archaeologists from INA and from Turkey's Museum of Underwater Archaeology at Bodrum. For years archaeologists have used local sponge divers as their eyes underwater. Within days, experts examined the wreck. They decided she was a Bronze Age ship. Judging from the copper ingots and other finds, she dated to about the 14th century B.C.

Why the wreck occurred may never be known with certainty, but it is possible that the ship was sailing to the northwest, directly against the prevailing summer winds. Because her sail was square-rigged, her crew would have had to tack in such conditions, following a zigzag course that might have taken her fatally close to land. Struck by a sudden gust, she could have staggered against wind and wave, her big sail flapping, her hull drifting uncontrollably toward the jagged rocks of Uluburun. Alternatively, an unexpected south wind could have been strong enough to dash her against the promontory.

Archaeologists Cemal Pulak and Donald A. Frey investigated the wreck with INA founder Jack Kelley in 1983. The ship, with copper ingots and huge storage jars, was an underwater archaeologist's dream, a time capsule of artifacts from all over the ancient eastern Mediterranean. She went down at a time when Egyptian pharaohs and Hittite kings competed for control of coastal sea routes. About 50 feet long, the Uluburun ship was typical of her breed, a coaster designed for durability, with short mast and a single square sail. She plied centuries-old sea-lanes that linked the Nile with the port cities of what are now Syria, Lebanon, and Israel. She also linked copper-rich Cyprus with Crete and mainland Greece. Pulak and archaeologist George F. Bass, who led the initial excavations, realized that the ship was a priceless archive of a vanished Bronze Age world. They started their excavations with key questions in mind: When did the shipwreck occur? Where had the vessel come from? What could the cargo reveal about the crew and trade relations of the day?

Contrary to popular belief, underwater archaeology involves far more than lifting amphorae and ship's timbers from the seabed. A month's diving meant two years' work ashore in laboratory, library, and museum. This particular wreck was especially demanding technically, for the ship lay at the foot of the Uluburun cliffs, on a steep slope; its wreckage had spilled over the seabed from 140 to 200 feet below the surface. At such depths, conventional scuba diving is limited in time, with nitrogen narcosis often clouding divers' minds. Between 1984 and 1994, 22,413 dives and 6,613 hours of excavation revealed a cargo of dazzling wealth, perhaps a royal payload.

Before anything was moved, teams of divers drew a plan of the wreck, as well as sectional profiles. These and the surviving two-inch-thick planking helped Cemal Pulak reconstruct the lines of the ship. A specially designed, handheld acoustic measuring device provided accurate positions for such objects as the 24 stone anchors that had been on board.

The vessel carried mostly raw materials, including ten tons of copper ingots and nearly a ton of tin, packed against branches of thorny burnet to protect the hull from the heavy cargo. That much metal could have made enough bronze helmets, corselets, spearheads, and swords to equip an army. Where had it come from? Pulak and his colleagues turned to high-tech sourcing techniques for help. Noel Gale, at the University of Oxford, used lead-isotope analysis on the Uluburun copper. The lead content closely resembled that from outcrops on nearby Cyprus, a major copper source during the Late Bronze Age. Tin, especially valuable in the ancient world, has proved much harder to source. Gale is just beginning to apply lead-isotope analysis to identify the geographical source of the tin ingots. George Bass believes the Uluburun tin came from Afghanistan.

Which way was the ship traveling? A large clay storage jar had tipped over and spilled a load of tightly stacked Cypriot pottery onto the seabed. Perhaps her home port was on Cyprus, but she also carried Canaanite amphorae and large Mycenaean or Minoan jars from mainland Greece or Crete. Perhaps the most definitive artifacts were some faience cylinder seals, widely used in northern Mesopotamia and Iran between 1450 and 1350 B.C. Seal expert Dominique Collon, of the British Museum, believes they may have originated near the city of Ugarit, now Ras Shamra, on the Syrian coast. Based on these artifacts, Bass and Pulak think the ship was voyaging from east to west, taking advantage of well-traveled routes that led from the eastern Mediterranean coast to Cyprus, then hugged the southern Turkish coast to the Aegean Islands and the Greek mainland.

At some point, perhaps near southern Italy, the ship headed across to North Africa, then followed the desert shore east to the Nile. There she may have picked up some of her most exotic cargo: logs of African blackwood, which the ancient Egyptians called *hbny* and used to fashion Tutankhamun's funerary bed. The skipper also acquired some scrap gold, including a broken Egyptian ring and a well-worn scarab inscribed with the name of Queen Nefertiti. This enabled Bass and Pulak to date the ship even more closely, for the queen died in about 1330 B.C. If the scarab was scrap, then the ship foundered no earlier than that date. They also made a seemingly prosaic (but fortunate) discovery in a piece of firewood bearing tree rings that dated to 1316 B.C., plus or minus two years. As for the crew, they may have come from the port of Ugarit, for their lamps were invariably of Syrian design.

*U*nderwater *archaeology, today: Totally mobile, this scuba diver fastens a hitch around a clay jar that once held oil or water aboard H.M.S.* Pandora. *The ship was carrying 14* Bounty *mutineers in manacles when it came to grief in 1791 on Australia's Great Barrier Reef. Before moving anything to the surface,* Pandora's *excavators plotted the position of every known artifact and ship's timber strewn across the seafloor.*

C*hanging pottery styles signal ancient changes in empire and in international trade. For centuries, travelers between ancient Egypt and Canaan favored a coastal route known to Egyptians as the Ways of Horus, often pausing at what is now Deir el-Balah, in the Gaza Strip.*

Modern excavations there, led by Israeli archaeologist Trude Dothan, chronicle six different strata, each containing potsherds relating to a different period. The lower three levels mark a time of powerful Egyptian influence; the upper three document successive occupations by Philistines, Israelites, and Byzantines.

The Uluburun ship carried a truly international cargo. Her manifest included Baltic amber from northern Europe, exotic wood from Africa, even tiny opercula—buttonlike plates from the feet of mollusks—that perhaps were to have been processed into incense. Archaeobotanist Cheryl Haldane Ward studied thousands of plant remains from the wreck. She identified seeds of coriander, black cumin, figs, grapes, and sumac; olives and olive pits; and pomegranate skins and seeds. About a ton of golden yellow resin from terebinth trees once filled the Canaanite amphorae. A small vessel of another highly aromatic resin also turned up, as well as charred grains of wheat and barley. One jar containing pomegranates also held tiny wood fragments. Cemal Pulak pieced the wood together into a folding writing tablet known as a diptych, once containing wax writing surfaces. Two wooden leaves with recessed inner surfaces were joined with an ivory hinge, forming a tiny book.

The Uluburun diptych is 600 years older than the earliest previously known example, found at the Assyrian palace of Nimrud in northern Iraq. Royal scribes there had mixed wax with 25 percent orpiment (arsenic trisulfide) to give it the right consistency and color. The Uluburun ship also carried quantities of orpiment. Archaeologists Michael Pendleton and Peter Warnock used a scanning electron microscope and modern timber databases to identify the wood of the diptych as boxwood. This easily worked wood was native to northern coastal Syria and Cyprus, which lay along the route the Uluburun ship is believed to have taken.

Few undersea archaeological discoveries rival this one, which has surrendered artifacts from at least ten cultures. Usually, only the more durable trade commodities manage to survive their long journey through time in recognizable form. Containers often outlast their far more perishable contents: olive oil, spices, wine. Trade in olive oil and wine reached near-industrial proportions in Roman times. A Roman wine carrier that sank off Madrague de Giens, France, near Marseille, carried thousands of wine amphorae padded with heather and rushes; some of the vessels were still sealed when they were discovered.

Until recently, our only knowledge of early manufacture of olive oil and wine came from written records. Egyptian tomb reliefs from about 3000 B.C. show the steps of winemaking. *The Epic of Gilgamesh*, a Sumerian text, describes a particular vintage as a "drink which was meet only for a king." Archaeologist and chemist Patrick E. McGovern, of the University of Pennsylvania Museum, launched a search for chemical traces of the original contents of ancient pottery vessels. Tartaric acid occurs in naturally high concentrations only in grapes; accumulations of its various residues on the bottoms of jars are a good indication that those jars once held wine. In 1990 McGovern and a colleague analyzed the residue from a 5,500-year-old storage vessel found in a trading post at Godin Tepe, in west-central Iran, and declared it to be the world's earliest known wine.

Thirty years ago, Mary M. Voigt—now at the College of William and Mary—discovered six pottery jars in the kitchen of a mud-brick building in the northern Zagros Mountains. They proved to be more than 7,000 years old. In 1996 McGovern and two colleagues analyzed residues retrieved from two of those jars, using infrared spectrometry, high-performance liquid chromatography, and sensitive wet chemical tests. They found not only high levels of tartaric acid, but also resin from the terebinth tree.

Ancient winemakers often added terebinth resin to their products, since it inhibits the growth of the bacteria that turn wine into vinegar.

By 5500 B.C., Near Eastern cultures had developed a distinctive wine technology that went far beyond merely allowing wild grapes to ferment naturally at room temperature. There were wine drinkers long before Giza's Pyramids rose by the Nile, long before Sumerian Ur became one of the great cities of the ancient Near East.

Uluburun shows us how artifacts mirror peoples' daily lives and reflect human relationships. Some relationships were strictly commercial, where one community exchanged volcanic glass for tropical bird feathers, or copper ore for grain or fine ornaments. In other instances, important leaders, often called "Big Men" by anthropologists, maintained regular links with one another by exchanging symbolic gifts. The obligations expressed by these gifts acted as an umbrella for extensive trade in food and other basic commodities.

Early in this century, pioneer anthropologist Bronislaw Malinowski studied the *kula* trade of the Trobriand Islanders, east of New Guinea. He observed how certain individuals continuously exchanged shell bracelets and necklaces with neighbors on other islands, according to traditional rules and routes of exchange. Holders of kula ornaments acquired great prestige, because the shells were valued symbols of trading connections that had persisted for generations. Some still endure to this day.

Two thousand years ago, the Ohio Valley was the center of the Hopewell complex, remarkable for its flamboyant burial customs and for far-flung trading. Dozens of communities exchanged exotic raw materials. Native copper came from Lake Superior and the Southeast; silver from Ontario; mica, quartz crystal, and chlorite from the southern Appalachians. Hopewell networks also dealt with marine shells from coastal Florida, galena from Illinois and Missouri, nodular flint from Illinois and Indiana. Obsidian came from the distant Yellowstone area of the Rocky Mountains; chalcedony from the Knife River region of North Dakota. Raw materials were fashioned into finished objects such as ceremonial copper axes and cutout silhouettes— in copper or mica—of birds, fish, claws, human heads and hands. We know these things from Hopewell burial mounds, where prominent individuals were placed in log-lined crypts within charnel houses or sacred enclosures. The bones of the departed were covered with earth for a considerable period of time; later, perhaps when an enclosure was full, the mourners dismantled or set fire to the houses, then heaped up basketfuls of earth to form a large mound over the dead.

Some individuals in the burial mounds may have been expert artisans, like one from the Hopewell site who was buried near 3,000 mica sheets and almost 200 pounds of galena. Another was interred with nearly 300 pounds of obsidian. Prominent people, such as a couple in the main

A

Altar

Washing
textiles

B

Backstrap-loom
weaving

C

Dyeing
yarn

C

Mass burial

MERCHANTS'
BARRIO

Spinning
yarn

San Juan
River

Pyramid of
the Sun

Looted
shaft
tomb

mound at Hopewell, went to the world of their ancestors adorned in such finery as copper earspools and breastplates. Hopewell archaeologists believe that many artifacts were formal gifts that held ritualistic and social meaning, gifts that linked communities in a common cosmology.

With cities and civilizations came caravans and trade routes across land and sea; beasts of burden and ships passed, independent of political developments along the way. For centuries, caravans of heavily laden donkeys crisscrossed the Syrian desert between various Assyrian cities in Mesopotamia and the strategic city of Kadesh, in Syria. There was even an Assyrian marketplace on the outskirts of that city. Cretan traders regularly visited Egyptian ports, even the royal court at Thebes.

The great cities of the past were as cosmopolitan as their modern equivalents. Medieval Cairo was a hub for caravans from all over western Asia and the Sahara. Chinese and Indian merchants lived in the Khmer cities of present-day Cambodia as early as 15 centuries ago. But only rarely do traces of such long-term visitors appear in archaeological sites.

Teotihuacan was the center of the Mesoamerican world in A.D. 500. Its barrios were home to people from a wide area. Evelyn Rattray, of the Universidad Nacional Autónoma de México, has excavated a neighborhood on the city's eastern side, where immigrants from the Veracruz region had lived for many generations. They built circular adobe houses with thatched roofs, identical to those of their Gulf Coast homeland. Rattray found mass burials and hundreds of Maya vessels bearing their distinctive orange, brown, and cream anthropomorphic designs. The inhabitants processed and wove fiber and yarn. They probably traded in exotic tropical luxuries such as cacao beans, rubber, and quetzal feathers.

On the western edge of the city, University of Western Ontario archaeologist Michael Spence excavated a barrio that once housed Zapotec traders from the area of Monte Alban in the Valley of Oaxaca, 250 miles south of Teotihuacan. These foreigners lived in the city's standardized housing, but their characteristic Zapotec pottery linked them to their distant homeland. Like the Veracruz traders, they followed their own burial traditions, depositing the dead within walk-in tombs. Apparently, native Teotihuacanos tolerated such foreigners in their midst because, as traders, they were economically important. Potsherds from their segregated barrios allow us to identify their presence in the crowded metropolis.

Every artifact from the past has a tale to tell, whether it belonged to a great king or a humble farmer. We can only guess at some of these stories, at the incredible journeys some must have involved. What stories my four red glass beads could share: Of a weeks-long journey in the arms of the monsoon, crossing the Indian Ocean by dhow; of a wearying, humid trek along the banks of the Zambezi River. First they resided in a huge string. But gradually the traders' bundles grew ever smaller, the strings shorter. Smaller and smaller lots passed from sweaty hand to sweaty hand until, finally, just four beads adorned the neck of a young man in a small village 4,000 feet above sea level.

The story of ancient trade relies on deciphering messages that come with thousands of such artifacts. From them we begin to understand the extraordinary webs of commerce that have linked various peoples, ever since anatomically modern humans first hunted on the African savanna.

Exploded view of the Merchants' Barrio on the outskirts of Teotihuacan proves that this metropolis of highland Mexico drew traders from afar. Tropical luxuries such as cacao beans, rubber, and quetzal feathers must have fetched good prices in Teotihuacan. Evidence of mass burials (A) and of abundant imported pottery (B) indicates that the builders of these circular adobe homes were from lowland Veracruz. Inhabitants of this long-established community worked fibers into fabrics (C).

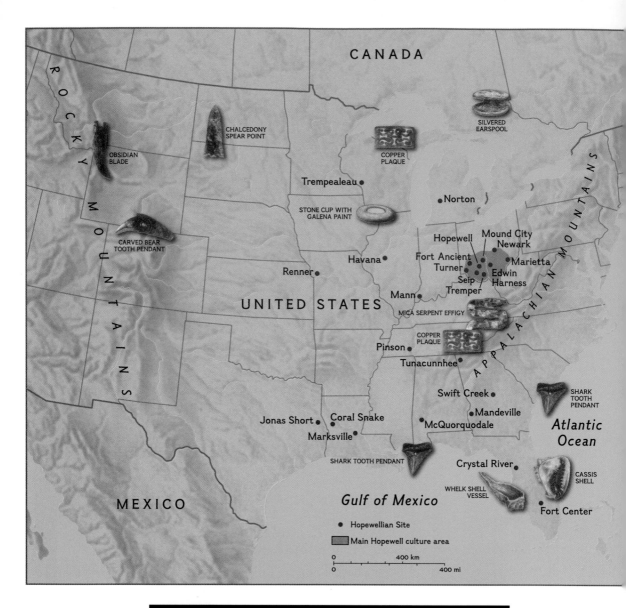

killed traders and artisans, the Hopewell people of Ohio exchanged raw materials over enormous distances early in the first millennium A.D. (opposite, map). For spear points, they imported obsidian from the Yellowstone area, also chalcedony from the Knife River region of North Dakota. The Florida coasts yielded abundant seashells; Lake Superior and the Southeast provided copper. Traders obtained silver from Ontario and sheets of mica from the southern Appalachians. A mica bear figure (opposite) may have symbolized a particular Hopewell clan.

Despite their expertise in trading, the Hopewell never built cities. Most lived in small villages and homesteads, governed by clan leaders of high rank. Each kin group lavished care on its honored dead, burying them in wooden charnel houses and later dismantling or burning the houses and covering the remains with earth.

A Newark, Ohio, golf course (above) overlies a 20-acre circular earthwork, part of a group of mounds and geometric enclosures built before A.D. 300. In such complexes of circles, squares, and octagons—sometimes joined by causeways—the Hopewell people once may have held solstice ceremonies and other celebrations.

A bird claw fashioned from translucent mica (right) expresses the significance of the natural world. Animal totems were important in Hopewell society, as they have been in other Native American cultures.

R emnants of the storied Silk Road—a network of caravan routes—linger in Xinjiang's Taklimakan Desert in northwestern China. Sands have all but swallowed the ruins of Niya (far right), a city that prospered for 500 years before dying at the end of the third century A.D. The timbers of one structure, illuminated during a time exposure, take on a ghostly glow (bottom).

Powerful kingdoms flourished along the Silk Road, and cities such as Niya arose along rivers that once flowed through the surrounding Tarim Basin. At least one archaeologist believes that settlement pressures upstream from Niya eventually caused water supplies to dry up, forcing inhabitants to move.

Carvings on a small wooden door from Niya (above) reflect a cosmopolitan society well aware of Indian elephants and mythical beasts of distant cultures. Some of the city's more prosperous residents furnished their reed-and-post dwellings with carved furniture that showed Greek and Roman influence. A Niya bowl (below) bears a symbol of a moving sun, perhaps indicating Mithraic worship,

which was commonplace in the Roman Empire during the second and third centuries.

British archaeologist Sir Aurel Stein mapped 20 square miles of Niya in the early 1900s. In addition to locating scattered remains of houses, he found two kinds of wooden documents (bottom right), both covered in Kharoshthi script, an Indian alphabet of Aramaic origin that was commonly used in Silk Road transactions. Narrow wooden strips carried routine messages, while the boxy, tamperproof wooden envelopes—tied with string and sealed with wax— held confidential letters.

A disaster 33 centuries ago but an archaeologist's dream today, the remains of a Bronze Age merchantman qualifies as the world's oldest known shipwreck. Laden with goods from all over the Mediterranean, she went down off Uluburun, Turkey, in the late 14th century B.C. Finds from the wreck range from a golden falcon pendant (right) to workaday items.

An Egyptian tomb painting from the same era, depicting the arrival of a Syrian fleet, helped NATIONAL GEOGRAPHIC artists re-create what the lost ship may have looked like (above). A large storage jar awaits unloading, while laborers carry four-eared copper ingots and unpack bronze-tipped spears. A bearded Canaanite merchant and a Mycenaean Greek admire a chalice of gold.

Belowdecks, the ship holds a layer of ballast stone covered with thorny burnet, a shrub used to cushion the valuable cargo. Bronze swords and arrowheads, Mycenaean

pottery, and ostrich eggshells lie at the stern. The center holds fishing nets, ingots of copper, tin, and blue glass, exotic wood, and resin-filled amphorae, all flanked by storage jars. Stone anchors, in pairs, lie forward of the mast.

At a depth of 150 feet, a Turkish excavator cleans debris from one of some 350 copper ingots (far left). Altogether, ten tons of copper and one of tin were aboard. At times the meals of the excavators were remarkably similar to typical Bronze Age fare (right): round loaves of bread, also cheese, chickpeas, garlic, goat meat, olives, figs, and fish.

Well-traveled trade routes of the Mediterranean come alive, thanks in part to the cargo found in the Uluburun wreck. Excavators George F. Bass and Cemal Pulak believe the ship was bound from Syria-Palestine to Cyprus, then to the Aegean, before returning by North Africa and Egypt. Sourcing analyses tell us the copper it held originated in Cyprus; the tin may be from Afghanistan.

Eared ingots, one of copper grouped with various bronze swords, spearheads, and cutting tools (below), allowed easy stacking, also transport on a donkey's back. Other exotic trade goods included ebony-like wood from Africa, amber from the Baltic, elephant and hippopotamus ivory, and ostrich eggshells.

Blue glass ingots (bottom center) were chemically identical to glass from Egypt and Mycenae, which shared similar manufacturing procedures (bottom right): After wrapping molten glass around an inert core, makers wound a second glass color over the first, then reheated the surface and worked it to create designs. Handles, rim, and foot were added before the core was broken and carefully removed through the vessel's mouth.

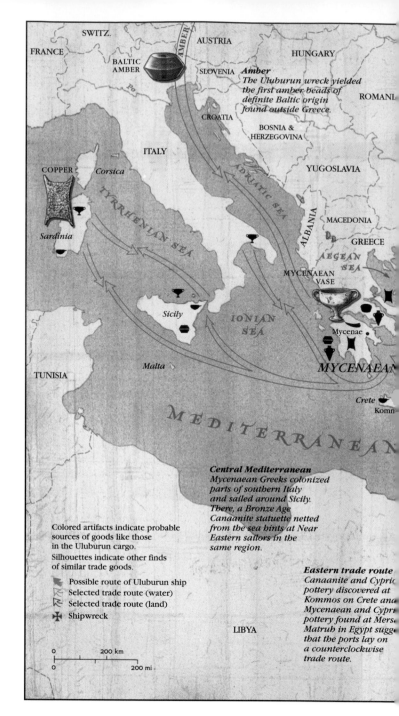

Amber
The Uluburun wreck yielded the first amber beads of definite Baltic origin found outside Greece.

Central Mediterranean
Mycenaean Greeks colonized parts of southern Italy and sailed around Sicily. There, a Bronze Age Canaanite statuette netted from the sea hints at Near Eastern sailors in the same region.

Eastern trade route
Canaanite and Cypriot pottery discovered at Kommos on Crete and Mycenaean and Cypriot pottery found at Mersa Matruh in Egypt suggest that the ports lay on a counterclockwise trade route.

Colored artifacts indicate probable sources of goods like those in the Uluburun cargo.
Silhouettes indicate other finds of similar trade goods.

⚓ Possible route of Uluburun ship
↰ Selected trade route (water)
↰ Selected trade route (land)
✠ Shipwreck

0   200 km
0   200 mi

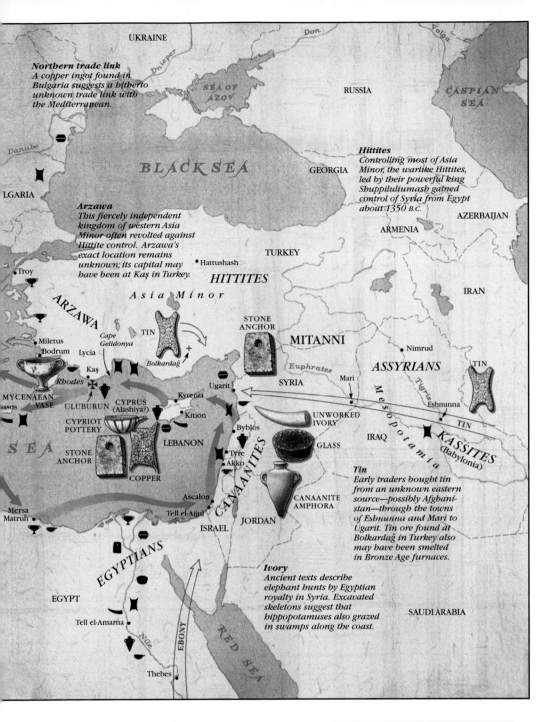

UKRAINE

Don

Dnieper

Volga

SEA OF AZOV

RUSSIA

CASPIAN SEA

Northern trade link
A copper ingot found in Bulgaria suggests a hitherto unknown trade link with the Mediterranean.

Danube

BLACK SEA

GEORGIA

Hittites
Controlling most of Asia Minor, the warlike Hittites, led by their powerful king Shuppiluliumash gained control of Syria from Egypt about 1350 B.C.

AZERBAIJAN

ARMENIA

LGARIA

Arzawa
This fiercely independent kingdom of western Asia Minor often revolted against Hittite control. Arzawa's exact location remains unknown; its capital may have been at Kaş in Turkey.

TURKEY

• Hattushash

IRAN

• Troy

ARZAWA

Asia Minor

HITTITES

TIN

STONE ANCHOR

MITANNI

Nimrud •

ASSYRIANS

TIN

Cape Gelidonya

Bolkardağ

Miletus
Bodrum

Lycia

Kaş

Euphrates

Mari •

Tigris

Mesopotamia

Eshnunna •

TIN

Rhodes

MYCENAEAN VASE

ssos

ULUBURUN

Ugarit

SYRIA

CYPRUS (Alashiya?)

Kyrenia •

• Kition

CYPRIOT POTTERY

LEBANON

Byblos •

UNWORKED IVORY

GLASS

IRAQ

KASSITES (Babylonia)

TIN

STONE ANCHOR

COPPER

SEA

CANAANITES

Tyre •
Akko •

Ascalon

Tell el-Ajjul

ISRAEL

JORDAN

CANAANITE AMPHORA

Tin
Early traders bought tin from an unknown eastern source—possibly Afghanistan—through the towns of Eshnunna and Mari to Ugarit. Tin ore found at Bolkardağ in Turkey also may have been smelted in Bronze Age furnaces.

Mersa Matruh —

EGYPTIANS

EGYPT

Tell el-Amarna

Nile

EBONY

RED SEA

Ivory
Ancient texts describe elephant hunts by Egyptian royalty in Syria. Excavated skeletons suggest that hippopotamuses also grazed in swamps along the coast.

SAUDI ARABIA

Thebes •

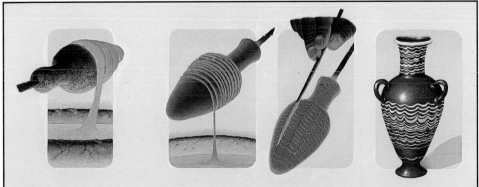

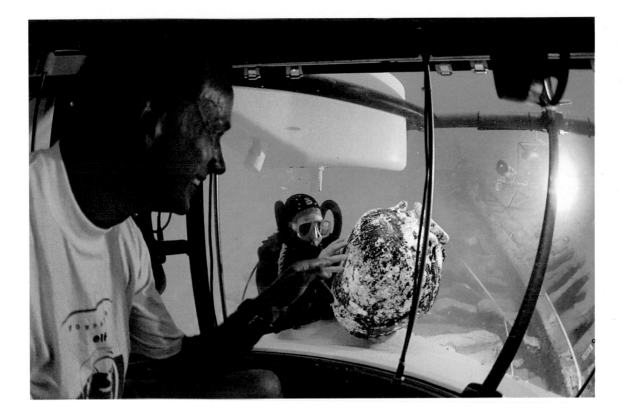

L aden with treasures from both the New and Old Worlds, the Spanish galleon Concepción *drifted onto the Silver Bank reef north of the Dominican Republic in 1641. An eroded copper "frothing pot" and a silver pitcher filled with hot chocolate stand next to other finds from the wreck (opposite). The silver spoon with mother-of-pearl bowl adds chocolate chunks to heated milk, stirred with a "frother." The round box may have held spices.*

Conservators painstakingly reconstructed an ornately decorated, 17th-century Chinese serving dish (right), made especially for export and found with Concepción.

At the wreck site of another galleon, the San Diego—*sunk off the Philippines in 1600— expedition leader Franck Goddio (above) rides a two-person submersible toward a diver with a stoneware jar.*

Cornerstone of the
Maya world, trade—over both
land and water—sustained
various Maya kingdoms. A
wealthy merchant in a litter
and his entourage (above)
parade serenely across a
painted Maya vase, here
photographically "unrolled."
Merchants in Tulum, on the
Yucatan Peninsula of Mexico,
specialized in the export of
honey. One sampling of trade
goods (right) from Cuello,
in northern Belize, includes
cotton and cacao, often
exchanged for jade, shell,
or obsidian. Many Native
American groups flaked

obsidian into tools such as this arrowhead (below) from Wyoming. Panum Crater, in California's Inyo National Forest, was a ready source of volcanic glass (right). Today, researchers can link many ancient stone implements to their source quarries.

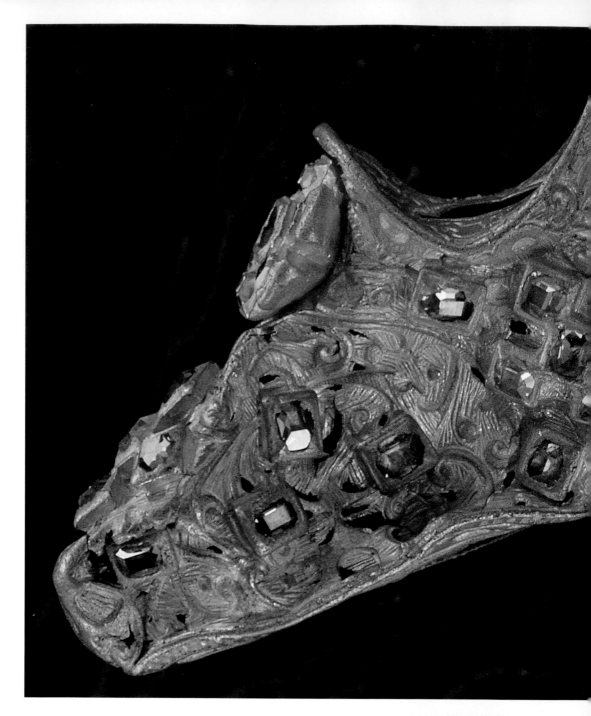

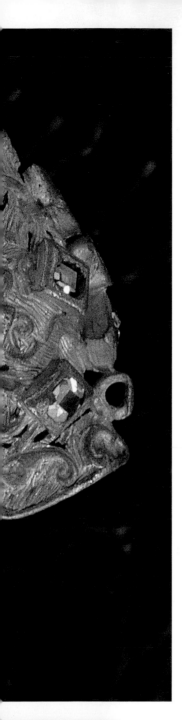

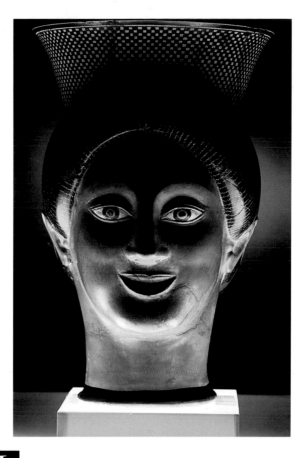

A round the world, in all cultures and all eras, objects both precious and practical have fueled trade and reflected various lifestyles of the times. This diamond-studded gold shoe pendant (left) may have originally contained exotic fragrances. It surfaced from the wreckage of the Manila galleon Nuestra Señora de la Concepción, which came to grief among the Mariana Islands in 1638.

Across the Mediterranean, Greek and Etruscan traders competed vigorously for market share. A whimsical Etruscan vase found in Greece (above) dates to about 500 B.C. It provides insights into how people of that era looked, as well as what they liked in art.

A clay vessel from the Colima culture that flourished along Mexico's Pacific coast from 250 B.C. to A.D. 450 bears the likeness of a hairless dog (below, far left). It indicates that the Colima people possessed this breed, which is distinctive to Mexico.

University of San Diego anthropologist Alana Cordy-Collins believes that, by A.D. 750, traders coasting the Pacific shoreline on balsa rafts introduced the hairless canines to the Moche people of Peru.

Decorative glass beads such as these gleaned from an 18th-century sailing ship lost off Bermuda (left) were central to the Atlantic slave trade. African merchants and rulers exchanged human cargoes for the baubles, manufactured both in Asia and in Europe.

Evidence of ancient trading in scrap, this toga-clad Roman statue was one of many broken

pieces of diverse ages recovered in 1992 from the Adriatic off Brindisi, in southern Italy.

ody parts of bronze fill an archaeological morgue (below), attesting to a prosaic but apparently profitable trade among ancients: the recycling of metals. Italian archaeologists recovered an impressive array of bronze heads, arms, feet, and fingers that may have been aboard a ship that sank off Brindisi between the third and sixth centuries A.D. The male head at center resembles a well-known Hellenistic prince's statue in the National Roman Museum. Eventually it was matched to its original torso.

Conservator Erzsebet Lantos gently removes remnants of the original clay core from the prince's head (opposite), because sea salts accumulated in it over the centuries could further damage the already fragile bronze. Many believe the bronze scrap was on its way from the eastern provinces of the Roman Empire to a foundry in Italy.

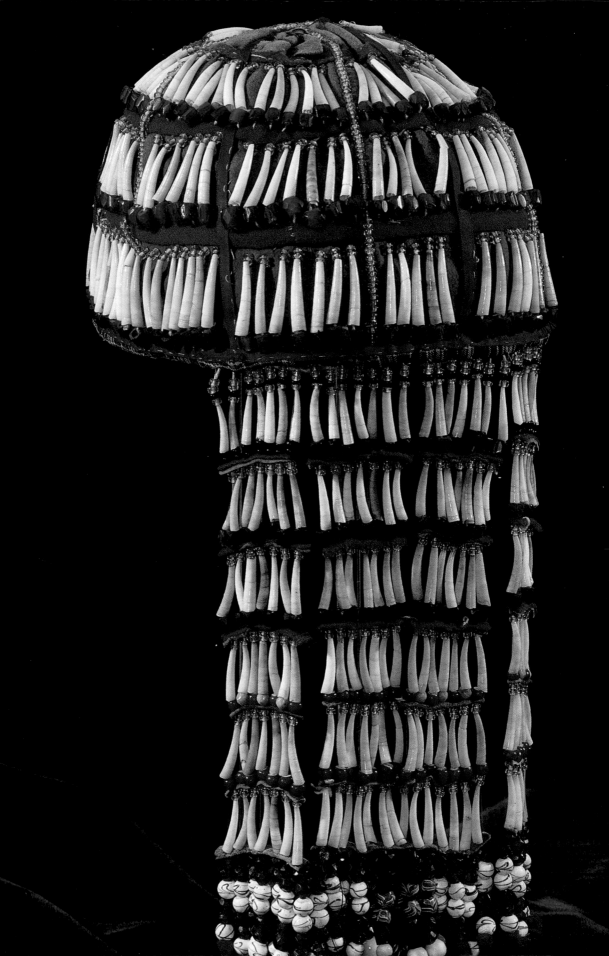

O ver time and in different cultures, money takes many shapes. Dentalium *shells were important symbols of wealth and power throughout western North America; the best came from the west coast of Vancouver Island, British Columbia. An elaborate ceremonial headdress of dentalia and beads (opposite) once adorned the wife of a Tlingit shaman in Klukwan, Alaska. The cap is made of green wool cloth, highlighted with red flannel and satin ribbons. The shell dress of the daughter of Oglala Sioux chief American Horse marked her as an important woman in 1908 (above).*

Of course, metal coins have served as currency in many civilizations. Bronze coins *(right, top) from the quake-ravaged Roman port at Kourion, Cyprus, date to the fourth-century reign of Emperor Valens.*

Some ancient currencies assume ritual significance and survive into modern times. Seashell ornaments used in the kula *trade (right) serve to unite distant individuals and different tribes of the Trobriand Islands, linking them in a centuries-old trade network. This Vakuta Island man prepares a shell armband for a ceremonial trading mission.*

Its pandanus-leaf sail filling to a gentle breeze, a Trobriand outrigger sets forth from

Kitava Island laden with shell ornaments that are part of the kula trade's endless cycle.

LIVES OF THE HUMBLE

The small Maya village of thatched adobe houses lay near a stream in El Salvador's fertile Zapotitan Valley, surrounded by growing crops. Each family lived in a group of buildings, with a small kitchen garden nearby. In the fields, farmers had doubled over the maize stalks to dry the ripe ears in the hot August sun.

Everyone had finished the evening meal. The dirty dishes still lay by the dying hearth fires. A scent of wood smoke wafted over the houses in the calm air.

A sudden rumble shook the village as an underground fissure less than a mile away erupted with little warning. Fast-moving clouds of ash and gases darkened the twilight sky. The villagers fled for their lives, leaving everything behind. Within minutes, their homes lay under a thick layer of

Tending to the staff of life, Egyptian bakers in an Old Kingdom bas-relief make bread by pouring dough into standardized clay pots (right) and covering them with clay tops that have been heated in an open fire (left).

A new generation of archaeologists now looks at the lives of ordinary folk, people whose history comes from everyday items, not from documents or the buried finery of the elite."

volcanic debris. Within a few days, the entire village was blanketed by more than 15 feet of ash.

Fourteen hundred years later, a bulldozer operator leveling the ground for grain silos accidentally uncovered the corner of a thatched structure mantled in ash. He had stumbled upon sixth-century Ceren, the Pompeii of the New World.

The eruption had unleashed hot lava bombs, which had set afire the thatched roofs of Ceren's houses. Many adobe walls had collapsed. But the rain of volcanic ash actually had preserved the contents of the village under a thick but relatively light overburden.

Like the Iceman or Tutankhamun's tomb, Ceren is an extraordinary archaeological treasure. We archaeologists excavate ancient settlements all the time. Almost invariably, the inhabitants abandoned them deliberately. Each family packed up its prized possessions and domestic utensils, perhaps set fire to its building or salvaged valuable roof timbers, then moved on. Ceren is different, a village frozen in a terrifying moment in time, with even finger smears inside food vessels preserved for posterity.

Payson Sheets, of the University of Colorado, is writing a story of households at Ceren, where husbands and wives, parents and children, perhaps in-laws and grandparents, all lived in close association. The people themselves are long gone, of course. We know neither their names nor the everyday details of their social interactions. Their artifacts and the remains of buildings and foods speak on their behalf, providing us with another form of archaeological conversation with the past.

Sheets enlisted a driver with an oxcart to run a ground-penetrating radar sensor over a field south of the bulldozed area. Such radar units send microwave energy deep into the soil and detect it as it is reflected back. By not using a motorized vehicle, Sheets ensured that the readings would be free of electrical and mechanical interference. Next he used a drill rig to sample irregularities picked up by the radar; some turned out to be hardened clay floors.

Then Sheets and his team used an electrical resistivity instrument to search for similar structures, assuming that hard adobe surfaces would offer less resistance to electrical waves than the blanketing ash. Some large, double- and triple-peaked anomalies turned out to be buildings.

Years of painstaking excavation and recording uncovered Ceren's houses. The excavators recorded every artifact, each wall fragment, even seeds and pieces of thatch. They plotted concentrations of finds, the telltale signs of families interrupted in the midst of their daily routines.

One household lived in a complex of four buildings: a kitchen, a workshop, a storehouse, and a residence where the inhabitants socialized, ate, and slept. The residence had a front porch open on three sides. Here a child may have played with a pile of 20 rounded potsherds, perhaps learning to count, using the Maya numerical system, based on 20. The

Momentarily recapturing one aspect of Egypt's distant past, assistant Abd al-Qadar heats the top halves of clay bread molds—made to an archaeologist's specifications—in an open fire (opposite). A National Geographic Society grant enabled archaeologists Zahi Hawass and Mark Lehner to build this outdoor bakery along the lines of an ancient one, as part of their investigation into Egyptian breadmaking practices. Using similar grains and yeasts that likely were available to Old

Kingdom bakers, their team produced dense sourdough loaves.

Half the world away at Ceren, El Salvador, three 1,400-year-old Maya serving dishes survived under an adobe bench (above) in a house that had been blanketed by volcanic ash. One bore finger marks from a long-ago meal.

main room covered 43 square feet, with storage pots against the back wall. One pot contained a spindle whorl for making cotton thread. The builders of the house had mounted handles from broken jars inside doorways, as hooks for tying the doors shut, and had also set them into some clay walls, as hangers. A large adobe bench on the east side of the room served as the sleeping place. During the day, people rolled up their mats and stored them among the rafters. An obsidian blade was found in the thatch overhead—a common local practice, both to keep sharp edges out of reach of children and to protect valuable tools from accidental damage.

A walkway that passed by a food-grinding area linked the dwelling to a nearby storehouse. A metate (bottom grinding stone) still stood on forked sticks, which elevated it about 20 inches above the ground. The woman who did the grinding must have been short! A well-tended garden adjoined the side of the storehouse. Here the women planted at least three species of plants, evidently medicinal herbs, in rows about three feet apart. Each plant stood in a small mound of soil. Just to the south, a field held ridges of young maize plants, 8 to 15 inches high, typical growth for August in this environment.

The Ceren excavations reveal humble Maya going about their daily business, the men working in the fields and making obsidian tools, the women weaving cotton garments, making agave rope and twine, and fashioning clay vessels. Theirs was a life dictated by the unchanging rhythm of the seasons, by rains and dry months, by the cyclical demands of planting and harvest. Families would gather for the evening meal, perhaps the only time when everyone was together. By chance, the volcanic ash rained down just after supper, so their artifacts preserve a chronicle of life at the end of a farmer's day.

Archaeological sites, whether villages like Ceren or great cities such as Sumerian Ur, are archives of human interaction. People lived and died in these places. They grew up, fell in love and got married, had children, quarreled with neighbors. These daily interactions—between women and men, rich and poor, foreign traders and locals, slaves and masters—are as much part of history as the deeds of kings and the conquests of generals. A new generation of archaeologists now looks at the lives of ordinary folk, people whose history comes from everyday items, not from documents or the buried finery of the elite.

Centuries after Ceren's demise, the Aztec would call Teotihuacan the Place of the Gods. Here Aztec deities took counsel and created anew the sun, moon, and the world. One of the fountains of Mesoamerican civilization, Teotihuacan arose at about the time of Christ, reached the height of its influence around A.D. 500, and lay in ruins 200 years later. Fifteen centuries ago, between 100,000 and 200,000 people lived in this eight-square-mile metropolis, which survived longer than most empires, ancient or modern.

We tend to think of ancient cities—and of the past in general—in terms of public structures: palaces, pyramids, and magnificent temples. But archaeology allows us to look behind the facade of fine buildings and lavish display, beyond the imposing Pyramid of the Sun and Pyramid of the Moon at Teotihuacan, into the humblest quarters of that great city.

Archaeologists René Millon, Bruce Drewitt, and George L. Cowgill mapped the Teotihuacan urban landscape in the 1960s. Millon called their project "a staggering undertaking," one that combined aerial mapping and photography with years of meticulous ground surveys. Millon and his colleagues walked every accessible plot of ground in the city. They mapped its great plazas and pyramids and identified about 2,000 apartment compounds. Teams of researchers collected thousands of figurines, nearly a million potsherds, and other artifacts. Together with photographs and maps, these finds created an archaeological portrait of a metropolis so large that it rivaled in size William Shakespeare's London—although it peaked a thousand years earlier.

Millon's Teotihuacan Mapping Project revealed the true extent of this long-dead city. The scientists discovered that beyond the ceremonial precincts had lain teeming barrios—neighborhoods—of single-story, flat-roofed, rectangular apartment compounds complete with courtyards and passageways. Each compound had been separated from its neighbors by straight streets about 12 feet wide and by narrow alleyways. Each had once housed between 20 and 100 people, most probably members of the same kin group. Some had sheltered skilled artisans, families who were expert obsidian or shell workers, or weavers, or potters.

Walking along a Teotihuacan street, I imagined passing down it 1,500 years earlier, bounded on either side by bare, plastered compound walls. Occasionally, a doorway would open into the street, offering a glimpse of a shady courtyard or textiles drying in the sun. But the smells and sounds would have told me much about the inhabitants: the clink of stone striking fine obsidian, the monotonous grating of maize being ground, the soft voices of women weaving, the smell of incense.

As I stood atop the Pyramid of the Moon, I tried to picture the living city that once had sprawled far beyond: thousands of flat apartment roofs

E veryday events in the lives of Copan's residents unfolded within sight of the city's temple-pyramids and public buildings. Humble folk farmed maize, beans, and squash, dwelling in thatch-roofed houses while tradespeople, artists, and nobles occupied more elaborate homes.

Today, a ten-square-mile chunk of fertile bottomland known as the "Copan pocket" encompasses some 3,500 mounds—the overgrown remains of ancient buildings— with more elsewhere in the Copan Valley. As many as 20,000 people lived at Copan during its heyday.

rimmed by a green patchwork of irrigation ditches and cornfields. I shut my eyes and sensed the smell of wood smoke, the shouts of street vendors, dogs barking, and the constant murmur of peoples' voices.

How can archaeologists be sure their reconstructions of such myriad activities are accurate? Part of the answer lies in the fact that excavators and surveyors using modern techniques have moved into the barrios, and researchers are finding traces of human activity even when artifacts are few and far between.

Linda Manzanilla, of the Universidad Nacional Autónoma de México, is part of this new generation of scientists. She has investigated a modest apartment compound in Oztoyahualco, near the northwestern edge of Teotihuacan. The apartments contained few archaeological objects, so Manzanilla and her team took samples from the stucco floors and analyzed them for chemical traces of various human activities. She developed a mosaic of different trace concentrations: Rotting garbage had produced high phosphate readings; dense concentrations of carbonate from lime—used in the preparation both of tortillas and stucco—indicated places where cooking had occurred or where stucco had been made.

Based on chemical analysis, Manzanilla's plans of the apartment complex are accurate enough to pinpoint the locations of cooking fires and places where the inhabitants ate such animals as deer, rabbits, and turkeys. Manzanilla was able to identify three nuclear families totalling about 30 people, who had lived in three separate apartments. Each had specific areas for sleeping, cooking, eating, and holding religious activities and funerary rites. Teotihuacan's barrios, like the houses of Ceren, have revealed intense interactions among people who knew each other well.

Artifacts sometimes tell stories of unspoken resistance and carefully preserved cultural identity. Three centuries ago in North America, for example, southern colonial plantations were kingdoms unto themselves. Each mansion was surrounded by acres of cotton, rice, or sugarcane; hundreds of slaves lived in shacks in the shadow of the big house. Their world was part of, yet entirely separate from, that of their masters.

Established in the early 18th century near Charleston, South Carolina, Middleton Place plantation was such a fiefdom, the imposing residence set amid formal gardens. During the Colonial and antebellum periods, generations of white planters prospered there. Their idyllic life ended in 1865 during the waning days of the Civil War, when General Sherman burned his way through South Carolina and destroyed all the buildings at Middleton, except the garbage-filled privy.

Archaeologists love privies. Their deep shafts (not unlike today's urban landfills) are layer cakes of domestic refuse that accumulated over many generations. While at the Institute of Archaeology and Anthropology at the University of South Carolina, Kenneth E. Lewis excavated through layers of trash in the Middleton Place privy. Some artifacts he found there mirror a time of conspicuous consumption and privilege.

Middleton's antebellum planters used expensive blue-and-white porcelain imported from China, as well as dishes with a pattern of delicate flowers called French Bourbon Sprig, popular both before and after the French Revolution. They poured from elaborately cut decanters and drank from fine stemware. Lewis also found many less elegant items in the privy, including some postbellum medicine bottles that indicate later residents suffered a variety of ailments ranging from upset stomachs to nervous conditions to night sweats associated with consumption.

The Middleton Place privy provides a skewed view, however, of plantation life. The far humbler artifacts and dwellings of a plantation's slaves tell a very different tale.

Thomas Jefferson, politician, philosopher, naturalist, and architect, was also a landowner, keeping as many as 220 slaves at Monticello, now preserved as a national shrine. But in Jefferson's day the estate looked very different. Some slaves lived along an access road called Mulberry Row, which contained 19 houses and workshops for slaves, artisans, and other hired help. These dwellings have not been preserved, but they have been investigated by William M. Kelso, who excavated Mulberry Row with the aid of Jefferson's own records. His dig confirmed the observation of a Jefferson contemporary that "the outhouses of the slaves and workmen… are all much better than I have seen on any other plantation…."

The artifacts found seem to indicate that a social hierarchy existed among the slaves. Some may have dined off fine ceramic plates, but most ate from humble earthenware bowls. Some enjoyed a richer diet than others, a fact we know by the animal bones found in the excavations. Buttons also turned up, apparently from clothes discarded by occupants of the main house. Kelso believes the slaves turned those garments into heavy quilts for their own use, stripping off the buttons in the process.

Leland Ferguson, of the University of South Carolina, has studied slave life at Middleburg Plantation, once a prosperous rice-growing enterprise in the South Carolina low country north of Charleston. He searched not for Middleburg's main house, which still stands, but for the humble, long-vanished slave quarters nearby. This plantation prospered from the early 1700s until 1861. Ferguson talked to local people, examined maps, searched archives and libraries, and eventually discovered the site of 12 "Negro Houses," dismantled more than a century ago.

The earth in his test pits yielded pieces of imported English ceramics and clay tobacco pipes, slave-made pottery, and the bones of many kinds of food animals. Middleburg was a trove of information about early African-American life, chronicling profound cultural differences between European-American colonists and their slaves. Digs of the slave quarters, for example, produced thousands of potsherds from handmade clay vessels baked in open fires, long known to archaeologists as Colono Ware—often shaped quite unlike those of local Native American vessels.

For decades experts had assumed Colono Ware was made by Native Americans, because slaves were anonymous figures in local history. But Ferguson recognized some shared characteristics between Colono Ware and African pottery. He also knew that, by 1740, blacks in South Carolina outnumbered whites almost two to one, and few Native Americans lived in the region. Fully a quarter of the blacks had been born in Africa. In effect, South Carolina was a black colony, much of it built with agricultural and craft skills imported from Africa.

Could Colono Ware have been slave-made pottery, manufactured using potting techniques learned thousands of miles away in West Africa? Ferguson examined complete Colono Ware vessels recovered from all manner of locations, including slave quarters, Indian villages, missions,

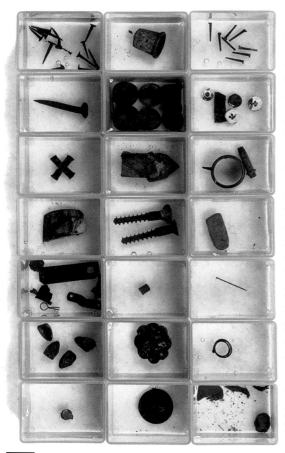

and plantation houses. Here, as elsewhere along the South's Atlantic coast, African women had arrived with a knowledge of potting; they used it to fashion domestic wares for their new homes. The widespread distribution of their distinctive unglazed earthenware, Ferguson realized, was the product of complex demographic and cultural forces, resulting from myriad interactions between blacks and whites as well as between both those groups and Native Americans.

Instead of just looking at pots, Ferguson also considered 18th- and 19th-century wood vessels and basketry—the entire "container environment" of the region. All three kinds of containers were broadly similar to those from the slaves' African homeland. Even the forms of bowls and other vessels mirrored the basic eating habits in Africa. In both areas, people used them for preparing and serving carbohydrates such as rice, millet, and manioc, with a vegetable relish or sauce on the side. Occasionally, small pieces of meat or fish were added.

Ferguson believes that African-American eating habits were quite similar to those of West Africans and radically different from those of the European Americans around them. He was struck by the remarkable similarities in Colono Ware over a large area of the South Carolina coast, all in an ethnic environment where close relationships with family and neighbors were vital to survival and where strong ties to ancestral African culture existed.

"*Small things forgotten,*" *archaeologist James Deetz calls the innumerable tiny artifacts that chronicle anonymous lives. The miscellaneous objects shown here belonged to a crew member of the Confederate ship C.S.S.* Alabama, *sunk off France in 1864 by the U.S.S.* Kearsarge. *More than 120 years later, divers working tide-scoured waters near Cherbourg recovered these items, which include bone buttons, nails, brass screws, and a thimble.*

Ferguson's research confirms that many African Americans retained aspects of their own culture despite being enslaved. In South Carolina and Georgia, slaves even spoke a distinctive African-American language. As their children grew up, they used earthenware bowls and other objects made by their elders and heard religious chants and stories of magic; these were some of the ways that the slave culture held on to its African roots, maintaining ideological power and molding the values of the young. While on a day-to-day basis many slaves could not alter the inferior social status bestowed on them by whites, prosaic artifacts such as earthenware pottery now speak of staunch adherence to pre-slavery values. Thus, archaeology offers telling clues of silent resistance to slavery and of the survival of traditional culture in the face of tremendous odds.

Archaeological research can also correct history. On the night of January 9, 1879, groups of Northern Cheyenne led by Dull Knife broke out of internment at Fort Robinson, Nebraska. They fought a running battle with the garrison, crossed the nearby White River, and headed up some bluffs into open country, where it took the military 11 days to recapture them. This much is beyond controversy. But what route did the Cheyenne take out of the river valley? According to military accounts, they moved up a conspicuous sandstone ridge to reach the bluffs.

Cheyenne oral traditions disagree. The presence of a full moon made such an exposed route illogical, even foolhardy. The Cheyenne version of the affair has always insisted that the Indians followed a well-protected drainage that offered excellent cover from pursuing riflemen.

Archaeologist Larry Zimmerman, when at the University of South Dakota's Archaeology Laboratory, decided to use a traditional field survey to check the oral tradition. His research team investigated the two escape routes with the collaboration of Northern Cheyenne representatives. They dug random test pits and used metal detectors to search for spent bullets in three areas—two sheltered drainages and the exposed ridge mentioned in military accounts. The surveyors recovered no bullets from the exposed ridge, but did find them in the streambeds, thereby confirming the oral account of the Cheyenne Outbreak.

This story may seem like a footnote to modern history, but the Northern Cheyenne struggle has become a classic tale of the American West, immortalized by John Ford's movie *Cheyenne Autumn*. The film portrays the Indians' escape from the perspective of the white victors. Now oral tradition and archaeology have joined forces, retelling history from the Indian point of view. In short, by scrutinizing an accepted historical "truth," science has given credence to a "myth."

Artifacts also tell remarkable tales about people who lived in the shadow of catalytic events in American history. The gold rush of 1849 was one turning point, transforming San Francisco from a quiet settlement into a booming city. William C. Hoff of New York was one of thousands of adventurers who flocked to California to seek fame and fortune. Hoff was different, for his dreams of wealth were realized not in the goldfields but in merchandising. Less than a year after his arrival, he founded a general store and ship supply house atop a busy waterfront pier in San Francisco.

Hoff's store went up in flames when the Great Fire of May 1851 engulfed the city. Hundreds of houses, hotels, and stores were lost in the conflagration. The charred remains of Hoff's store vanished under the streets of an expanding San Francisco, only to be unearthed more than a century later, during excavations for the foundations of a high-rise.

Archaeologist Allen G. Pastron spent nearly a year excavating the store's remains, some 15 feet below today's street level, recovering typical stock of a general store: salt pork, dried beans, and hardtack. He also found evidence for a wide range of finer foodstuffs: Truffles, oysters, coffee beans, walnuts, bottles of French champagne and Bordeaux wine, as well as butter and imported olives still in their jars. A miner could buy clothing and leather boots at Hoff's, also tin plates, utensils, and the tools of his trade.

Such humble objects help us experience the daily lives of ordinary men, women, and children. We can visualize their efforts to face life's challenges, whether from natural disasters, slavery, war, or economic struggles. The records are there, in the stained earth, in food remains, in other everyday artifacts. Such remnants tell us tales of the lives of the humble—stories that attest to the dignity of the human spirit, in difficult and often dangerous times.

Long-vanished houses of Mulberry Row—the accesss road to Monticello— once sheltered Thomas Jefferson's slaves and hired workers. More recently, the area has yielded a wealth of commonplace artifacts. A Jew's harp and part of a fiddle bow join dominoes and marbles; pencils and a fragment of an inscribed slate may testify to some degree of literacy among Jefferson's slaves.

Archaeologists search for ceramics and other household effects inside the root-embraced

foundation and earth-walled storage cellars of a house along Mulberry Row at Monticello.

135

Ancient Egyptians bring in the harvest, hauling baskets of ripe grain to the threshing floor as two youngsters fight over gleaning rights and nearby laborers take a break under a tree (above, lower panel). Driven oxen (upper panel) thresh the harvest while workers use wooden pitchforks to push grain under the hooves. Winnowers, their hair covered by linen dust shields, separate kernels from chaff with wooden

scoops—while the master oversees the final results.

A stone figurine (opposite, bottom left) turns grain into mash to make beer, a staple both for the living and the dead in ancient Egypt.

Miniature toys (below) from Pakistan's Indus Valley attest to the area's early success in domesticating animals. The diminutive ox at far left boasts a hinged head joined to the body with string.

Bedouin woman in Israel's Negev Desert prepares flat bread for baking over an open fire,

carrying on a tradition that has flourished throughout the Mideast for thousands of years.

Maize, gift of the gods: Puuc Maya farmer Santos Lopez harvests corn in Yucatan,

bending down stalks to protect the remaining ears from moisture as they dry.

ounty of the oceans has
fed nobles and commoners
alike, but only the humble
bring in that harvest. Ancient
Roman mosaic (opposite)
depicts fishermen using a
trident and an open boat to
bring in fish of all kinds.
Dozens of Roman fishing
communities dried their
catches or processed them
into fish sauce for growing
urban populations. The take
often included tuna and
squid, both Mediterranean
staples to this day.

As his ancestors have for
generations, a Polynesian
expertly spears a fish in
Aitutaki Lagoon (above),
in the Cook Islands. His
simple but effective method
enables him and other Cook
Islanders to bring in dozens
of fish an hour.

Islands in a sea of barrios ancient and modern, Teotihuacan's Pyramids of the Sun and the

Moon anchor some five square miles of old apartment compounds, most still unexcavated.

One-story compounds of plastered stone once made up the bulk of Teotihuacan's ancient barrios. Mexican archaeologist Linda Manzanilla excavated a multifamily apartment in the city's Oztoyahualco neighborhood (right). Three related families occupied separate, multiroom quarters. Judging from the tools found, some family members were plasterers (A). Others left behind the bones of rabbits they raised. A rabbit sculpture (B) stood on a ritual patio, perhaps the embodiment of a patron deity.

Often, people were buried with ritual offerings in graves under the floors (C). Thousands of small clay

figurines (above) littered this and other barrios in the city; some may represent common household gods or perhaps residents engaged in domestic ceremonies.

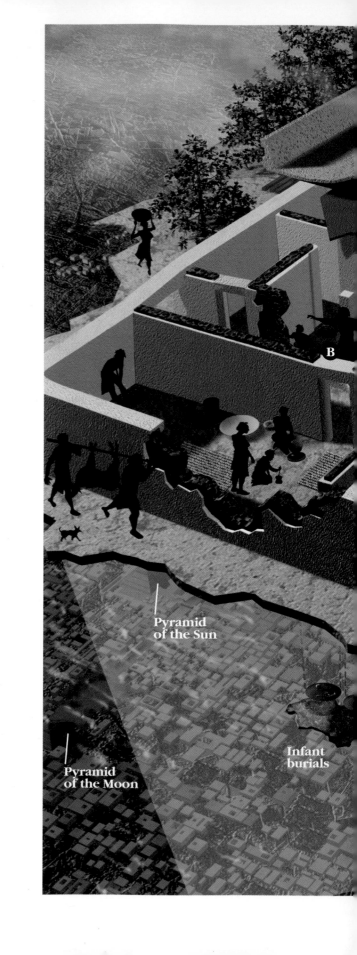

B

Pyramid of the Sun

Pyramid of the Moon

Infant burials

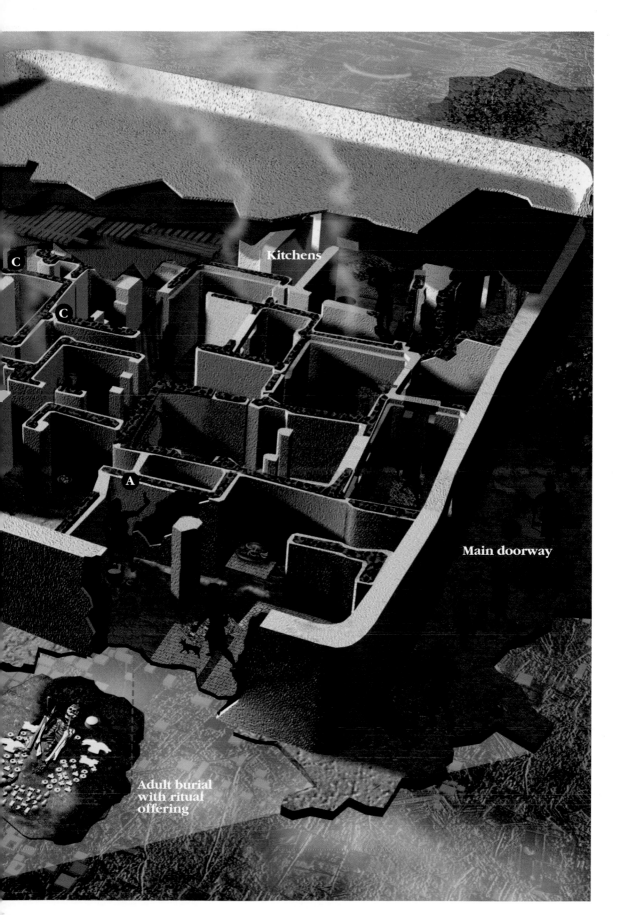

C

C

Kitchens

A

Main doorway

Adult burial
with ritual
offering

Anasazi art still emblazons the walls of a cliff dwelling at Cedar Mesa, southeastern Utah.

The shelter's design reflects basic priorities: easy defense and adequate maize storage.

MIRRORS OF THE
INTANG

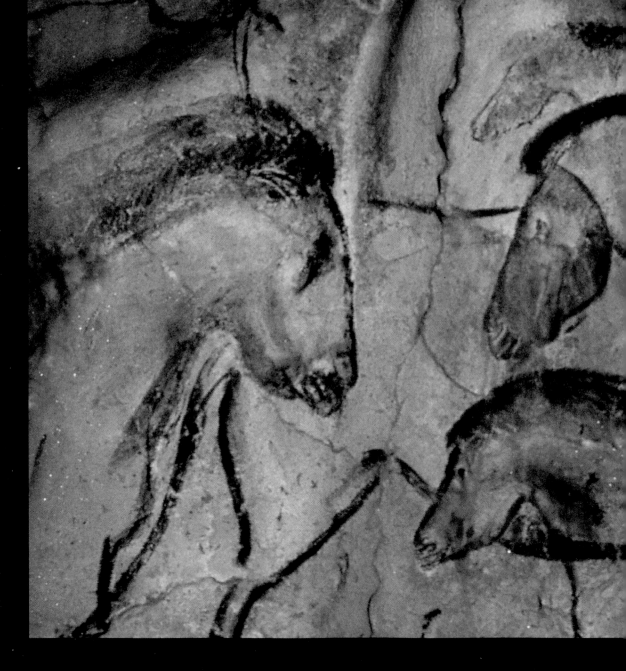

IBLE

"The past is a picture book without captions; the intangibles of human existence vanish with the owners."

"Mira, Papa, bueyes!" (Look, Father, oxen!) The excited words echoed through the chambers of Altamira cave in northern Spain in 1879. Don Marcelino Sanz de Sautuola's daughter María had insisted on tagging along on the excavations. Soon she had tired of the mud and dirt and had wandered off with a lamp to explore.

Grabbing a lantern, Sautuola crawled into the low side chamber where María was pointing at the roof of the cave. To his astonishment, red, brown, and black bison cavorted across the ceiling a few feet above his head.

At the World Exhibition of Paris the previous year, Sautuola had seen some engravings of Stone Age art. He was convinced the Altamira cave paintings dated from the late Ice Age, between 30,000 and 12,000 years ago. But the experts

Symbols of ancient rituals, 30,000-year-old wild horses parade on the walls of Grotte Chauvet, France. Paleolithic shamans painted the rear quarters of a feline over the horses, sparing their heads.

only laughed at his claims. Some even accused him of commissioning a forgery. Yet Sautuola was right. Eventually, other cave paintings came to light in deep caverns near Les Eyzies, in France's Dordogne, and in the Pyrénées, alas too late for Sautuola to be vindicated in his own lifetime.

Today, Altamira stands as one of the great masterpieces of late Ice Age art, painted more than 12,000 years ago. Until recently, few painted caverns rivaled it except Lascaux, near Montignac, on the Vézère River in France's Dordogne. Lascaux was discovered by adolescent boys in September 1940. In this underground cavern 17,000 years ago, a group of Cro-Magnon artists (named after the Cro-Magnon rock shelter near Les Eyzies) had painted great primordial bulls, deer, bison, and other formidable prey.

Altamira and Lascaux are the Sistine Chapels of the earliest art tradition in the world. Generations of archaeologists have gone deep underground in search of other undisturbed friezes, hidden since the late Ice Age. Few have ever had the deeply emotional experience of entering an undisturbed Stone Age cavern.

"The artists' souls and spirits surrounded us." Such was the testimony of Eliette Brunel-Deschamps, Jean-Marie Chauvet, and Christian Hillaire, three speleologists with an interest in archaeology who, on December 18, 1994, had crawled into a small opening in the Cirque de Estre gorge, deep in the Ardèche in southeast France. They were seasoned cavers, with years of experience searching for Ice Age paintings. But nothing had prepared them for what lay beyond that narrow defile.

They squeezed through the cramped entrance into a vestibule with a sloping floor and felt a draft coming from a heap of stones. They believed it might be a partially blocked duct. Pulling away the rocks from the opening, they discovered an extremely narrow passage, through which Brunel-Deschamps, smallest of the three, crawled with great difficulty. Then she saw a vast chamber 25 feet below. Using a rope ladder, the trio eventually lowered themselves into what turned out to be a network of chambers adorned with superb calcite columns.

What the world would soon know as Grotte Chauvet— Chauvet Cave—had lain undisturbed since the late Ice Age. Soot-blackened hearths looked as if their fires had been extinguished only the day before. The trio saw calcified bear bones lying on the floor, as well as shallow depressions where the beasts had hibernated.

Suddenly, Brunel-Deschamps cried out in surprise. Her lamp shone on two lines of red ocher, then the figure of a small mammoth. More mammoths roamed the walls farther in, also cave lions and painted prints of human hands. As the three explorers gazed at the paintings, they later wrote, they were "seized by a strange feeling. Everything was so beautiful, so fresh, almost too much so. Time was abolished, as if the tens of thousands of years that separated us from the producers of these paintings no longer existed." Like the excavators of the tomb of the Egyptian pharaoh Tutankhamun three-quarters of a century earlier, they felt like intruders.

On a second visit later the same day, they found an extraordinary frieze of black horses, wild oxen with twisted horns, and two rhinoceroses

Flickering firelight and boundless imagination illumine a Mohawk longhouse at Otstungo, near the Mohawk River (opposite). A tattooed storyteller gestures with a turkey-feather fan, while an artist carves an effigy pole.

A 500-year-old burial mound at Etowah, Georgia, yielded a ceremonial rattle in the form of a human head (below). Carved from wood and covered with thin copper sheet, the hand-size ornament was adorned with shell teeth. It may represent a supernatural being.

facing one another. There were also lions, reindeer, and bison. The horses had half-open muzzles; their eyes were depicted in detail. Before painting the animals, the artists apparently had scraped the wall to make them stand out, using contours and crevices to produce relief and perspective. In a nearby chamber, a bear skull lay atop a boulder. More than 30 calcite-covered bear skulls were scattered about.

Realizing they had discovered a cave that rivaled Altamira and Lascaux, Brunel-Deschamps, Chauvet, and Christian returned yet again on Christmas Eve with a few friends. Acutely conscious that the cave should be kept as it had been found, they laid plastic sheeting over their own footprints to encourage later visitors to stay on the same route. They also discovered an end chamber with another extensive frieze of black figures dominated by lions or lionesses, rhinoceroses, bison, and mammoths, with a horse right in the middle. To the right and facing the frieze stood a human figure with a bison head. They wrote that he "seemed to us to be a sorcerer supervising this immense frieze."

Before archaeologist and top rock-art expert Jean Clottes arrived at Grotte Chauvet, he doubted the paintings were genuine. But his skepticism vanished when he saw that many were covered by a layer of calcite, which takes many millennia to form. Questions raced through his mind: Had the bears used the cave before the humans? What was the relationship between the two? He estimated that at least 300 animal figures and numerous signs had been painted or engraved on the cave walls.

After careful stylistic comparisons with other cave art, Clottes guessed the Chauvet paintings might be between 17,000 and 21,000 years old. Archaeologists had had no means of dating rock art until 1983; conventional radiocarbon dating required about a handful of charcoal or other organic material for each test, which would have meant destroying an entire painting just to date it. But the development of a radiocarbon method based on accelerator mass spectrometry (AMS) had revolutionized the field, for it allowed technicians to date much smaller samples. Now, just a few tiny charcoal flecks from a single rock painting would suffice.

Clottes eagerly turned to this new technique in hopes of confirming his estimate. Surprisingly, the AMS dates of some Chauvet paintings indicated they had been executed over a 1,300-year period around 31,000 years ago—at least 10,000 years earlier than the original estimate—making them the oldest dated art in the world! Torch-charcoal smears on the walls dated to around 26,500 years ago, while two samples from the floor gave readings of about 24,000 years, and another one about 29,000 years. Clottes concluded that humans had visited Chauvet on several occasions during a span of at least 6,000 to 7,000 years. Whether they painted throughout that long period is still unknown, but AMS dating of paintings will ultimately produce answers.

Grotte Chauvet was also a bear cave, a place where these powerful animals had hibernated. Interestingly, many of the creatures depicted on Chauvet's walls represent the more dangerous members of the late Ice Age bestiary—bears, lions, mammoths, rhinoceroses, bison, also nimble and rather ferocious aurochs, as well as one panther. Clottes wondered if human visitors to the cave had come to the chambers to acquire the potency of the great beasts.

For nearly a century, archaeologists have argued over the meaning of Cro-Magnon art. Why did these late Ice Age people take flickering torches and animal-fat lamps underground, there to paint vivid depictions of animals surrounded by complex signs and, sometimes, handprints?

Judging from what we know of more recent hunter-gatherer groups, the Cro-Magnons enjoyed a close spiritual relationship with animals, plants, and the rest of the natural world. Human figures appear only rarely in their paintings; even so, they hint that shamans or sorcerers may have presided over ceremonies held in the caves, far from daylight.

In many cultures, shamans are believed to pass freely between the living and the spirit worlds, turning themselves into creatures such as bears or bison. Perhaps the painted caves were places where humans communicated with animal spirits that dwelled behind the rocky walls, somewhere in the supernatural.

Cro-Magnon paintings pose some of archaeology's great questions. They also provide a mute link between us and that faraway world of early humans—and the supernatural realm that surrounded them.

In the course of a lifetime, Stone Age hunter-gatherers probably encountered relatively few people outside their immediate groups. They spent most of their days within the small compass of their own families. Hunter-gatherer life was fluid, always in flux. Human groups split and fissured constantly, surviving by virtue of their very flexibility, even if there was constant tension within them.

Ten thousand years ago, the first farmers created an entirely new spiritual world, one that revolved less around game animals and more around fields and herds. Farming altered human life dramatically, changing people from nomads into permanent settlers who occupied small villages.

Human lives unfolded according to new rhythms and fresh imperatives, no longer according to the movements of game or the seasons of wild plants. Now they followed the ever unfolding cycles of planting and harvest, life and death. Time flowed in an endless cycle of seasons, with the land itself living and dying, just as human life flowed and ebbed in a constant passage from one generation to the next. People assumed their descendants would inherit the same world that they and their forebears had enjoyed. Such a view of life, of time itself, fostered close relationships between the living and the dead. As individuals died, they were elevated to the status of revered ancestors. This concern with one's ancestry goes back at least 8,500 years.

The plaster figures stared at me with serene, almost ghostly confidence. Androgynous, some more than three feet tall, they gazed wide-eyed across 85 centuries, as if possessed with boundless wisdom. I felt their eyes follow me around the room. I first saw these statues in the Smithsonian Institution's Arthur M. Sackler Gallery, in Washington, D.C. They had come from 'Ain Ghazal (Spring of the Gazelles), one of the earliest farming villages on earth, whose inhabitants lived between 7200 and 5000 B.C., only a few centuries after farming began, cheek by jowl with tethered goats in rectangular houses with carefully plastered floors.

An unknown number of similar statues had been destroyed in 1974, when a bulldozer operator carving out a road in the suburbs of Amman, Jordan, unknowingly cut through a buried collection of the figures. Ten years later, a team of archaeologists sifting through the bulldozed section came upon molded but crumbling pieces of plaster that resembled human forms, about eight feet below the surface. The team, led by Gary Rollefson of the 'Ain Ghazal Research Institute in Germany and Alan Simmons of the University of Nevada at Las Vegas, returned the following year to carry out a special rescue mission. Team members recovered the cluster of ritual objects. Since the plaster figures, lying face-up in a tight group beneath the floor of a house, were so fragile, the scientists decided to lift them and the surrounding soil in a single block.

The Smithsonian Institution's Conservation Analytical Laboratory in Suitland, Maryland, undertook the delicate task of disengaging the badly fractured statues from the matrix of soil. Fragments were analyzed by using X-ray diffraction and electron microscopy, then were strengthened with special chemicals. Conservators reconstructed the figures, solving three-dimensional jigsaw puzzles of limb and body fragments by using informed guesswork and precise measurements to fill in the gaps.

They also discovered that the 'Ain Ghazal artists of 8,500 years ago had started with armatures of twine-bound reeds. (Although the reed bundles decayed over time, their impressions survived on the interior surfaces of the plaster figures.) Each artist had then molded fine lime plaster over the reeds to form a torso, modeling buttocks, chest, legs, knees, and feet. Shoulders were lifelike, but the figures had no arms. Their long necks perched atop the bodies, supporting heads that bore calm, expressive faces and staring, incised eyes, inlaid with bitumen. Several torsos were given two heads; perhaps they memorialized husbands and wives, perhaps dual deities.

As I stared at the 'Ain Ghazal figures, something seemed familiar about them—they looked like department-store mannequins! With their square, stylized torsos and more realistic legs, it appeared quite possible that they once might have worn garments, perhaps cloaks or ceremonial gowns that covered their nonexistent arms. This might also explain recesses in the heads, which seem ideal for bearing headdresses or even flowing scarves. Speculation, of course, but plenty of historical analogies exist. The ancient Egyptians and Sumerians often clothed or painted statues of their deities. The cult statue of Athena on the Acropolis at Athens wore a magnificent saffron robe that took nine months to weave. To this day, some images in Roman Catholic churches and in Hindu temples wear different robes in different religious seasons. But who were the 'Ain Ghazal figures: gods, revered ancestors, or simply prominent individuals?

Three plaster masks from the same village, found in a separate shallow pit, date to before 7100 B.C. They have mouths that smile slightly;

their cheekbones stand out in delicately modeled, pinkish plaster. But their eyes are closed. They seem remote, almost otherworldly, emissaries from a vanished time and place. Their lifelike countenances stem from once living people, for they apparently were formed by pressing wet plaster onto skulls—a technique that provides a possible clue to similar finds from yet another cache of figures.

In the early 1950s, British archaeologist Kathleen Kenyon found human skulls with carefully plastered faces in the remains of a village as old as 'Ain Ghazal, at the base of the great Jericho city mound in the Jordan Valley. Like the 'Ain Ghazal masks, they had been preserved for posterity. Kenyon believed that mourners had either buried their dead or exposed the bodies until the flesh had decayed. Then they had preserved the skulls, molding faces in the likenesses of the departed, bestowing upon the deceased the standing of respected ancestor.

Perhaps the 'Ain Ghazal figures are manifestations of a similar ancestor cult, sexless depictions of those who went before. They stand timeless, supervising and validating the deeds of their descendants. Alas, we shall never decipher the innermost thoughts of the people of 'Ain Ghazal, for writing and literature were a few thousand years in the future.

The past comes to us as mute images. The departed speak to us through their artifacts, their art, and their architecture. In the absence of writing, we can only guess at their thoughts, their passions, their religious beliefs. The past is a picture book without captions; the intangibles of human existence vanish with the owners. We cannot hear our predecessors' laughter, their chants, their angry outbursts. We cannot argue with them about their political or philosophical beliefs. Fortunately, however, archaeology often brings their minds into sharper focus for us. Then the silent picture book acquires at least a few tentative words.

"Who shall read them?" wrote American travel writer John Lloyd Stephens of Maya glyphs he saw in 1839. Stephens assumed—correctly, as it turned out—that the intricate writings found in the rain forest held secrets of a long-forgotten ancient civilization. Today, his archaeological successors use the same glyphs to better understand the spectacular cities Stephens revealed to an astonished world. Archaeology and the successful translation of many glyphs has opened a gateway to the Maya cosmos.

More than 150 years ago, Stephens and English artist Frederick Catherwood arrived at the tiny village of Copan, in what is now Honduras, searching for the remains of a lost city. Stumbling through dense growth, the two men came upon a square stone column elaborately sculpted in bold relief. "The front was the figure of a man curiously and richly dressed, and the face, evidently a portrait, solemn, stern, and well fitted to excite terror," wrote Stephens. Large hieroglyphs adorned the sides of the stela.

Catherwood and Stephens followed their guide into the center of an overgrown city, the artist pausing occasionally to note a particularly fine relief. Trees and underbrush mantled Copan in brooding silence, broken only by the sound of monkeys moving through the branches, "in long and swift processions, forty or fifty at a time...." They passed a kaleidoscope of sculptures, plazas, and pyramids. "All was mystery, dark, impenetrable mystery," wrote Stephens. The city, once bustling, now was silent.

G
hostly chorus of hands congregates on the rocks along Argentina's Río Pinturas, the "river of paintings." Among the earliest dwellers of southern Patagonia, the Toldense people used their own hands as stencils between 7,000 and 9,000 years ago, spraying solutions of ocher and other minerals on the stone. Such paintings may have sought to draw powers from spirit forces thought to dwell within or beneath the rock.

While Catherwood, ankle-deep in mud, sketched stelae and wrestled with the complexities of the hieroglyphs, Stephens pondered the mysteries of the ancient city of Copan. Who were the richly decorated human figures that adorned at least 14 stelae? Were they foreign conquerors or the ancestors of modern Maya? John Lloyd Stephens declared roundly that Copan, Palenque, Uxmal, and other ancient Central American cities were "constructed by the races who occupied the country at the time of the invasion by the Spaniards...." Today, we know he was right.

Forty more years would pass before the Englishman Alfred Percival Maudslay traveled seven times through the Maya lowlands, making accurate copies of hieroglyphic inscriptions. Unfortunately, most experts of his day considered the glyphs merely pictorial depictions of the Maya calendar, not elements of a language. They assumed Maya rulers were peaceful priest-astronomers, obsessed with the movements of heavenly bodies and the passage of time.

Only Russian epigrapher Yuri Knorozov disagreed. In 1952 he argued that Maya glyphs formed a syllabic script. Knorozov based some of his research on the writings of the Franciscan friar Diego de Landa, who had traveled in Yucatan in the mid-16th century. Landa had destroyed priceless Maya documents, for religious reasons. Yet he had been a keen observer, recording some details of the Maya calendar and providing clues to their phonetic script in his book, *Relación de las Cosas de Yucatan*.

In the late 1950s Russian-born artist Tatiana Proskouriakoff was studying carved stelae at the ancient city of Piedras Negras, Guatemala, when she realized that the inscriptions were not only religious messages but also records of once living lords and their reigns. In Mexico, at Yaxchilan, she identified the history of Shield Jaguar and his son Bird

Jaguar, each with his own glyph symbol. Her discoveries came eight years after Mexican archaeologist Alberto Ruz Lhuillier had cleared a hidden stairway in the heart of the Temple of the Inscriptions at Palenque and uncovered a chamber containing the sarcophagus of a great Maya ruler wearing a jade mosaic mask. Intricate hieroglyphs and relief covered the five-ton stone slab over the tomb, but Lhuillier could not read them; neither could he decipher the name of the lord who lay below.

Building on the earlier work of Heinrich Berlin, a group of Mayanists gathered at Palenque in 1973 for a conference. In front of an astonished audience, epigrapher Floyd Lounsbury, art historian Linda Schele, and archaeologist Peter Matthews huddled over the Palenque glyphs, identified the standardized way in which rulers and their reigns had been set down, then laid out the life stories of six Palenque lords. The man buried under the Temple of the Inscriptions was none other than Pacal the Great, who ascended Palenque's throne in A.D. 615 and ruled for 68 years.

The decipherment of Maya script is one of the great scientific achievements of this century. Years of vigorous argument, controversy, and laborious translation have unraveled many details of Maya history, at least its public face. Monumental inscriptions tell of royal accessions, military victories, and important ceremonies. They show rulers in the presence of gods and royal ancestors, validating their authority as intermediaries between the people and the forces of the supernatural.

We now know Maya kingship passed from father to son, or from brother to brother to son, through long dynasties that extended back to an ancient founding ancestor. Political power came with genealogy—one's relationship to revered ancestors. Pacal's sarcophagus lid recorded his royal pedigree and his descent into the otherworld, even as it foretold his eventual resurrection, like the sun rising in the east.

Few Maya royal burials were as lavish as Pacal's. Although dozens of ceremonial centers dotted the Maya lowlands, only a handful—Calakmul, Copan, Palenque, Tikal—were large cities. La Milpa, on the western edge of what is now Belize, was founded by about A.D. 50 and abandoned some four centuries later, before enjoying a revival from 750 to 850. Never a first-level center, it clusters around a five-acre plaza dominated by four large pyramids.

While excavating that plaza, Boston University archaeologist Norman Hammond uncovered layers of limestone and flint chips filling a shaft. The shaft led to a burial chamber that had been carved out of solid limestone, about ten feet below ground level. The chamber, which Hammond compared to "the size of a Volkswagen bug," contained the skeleton of a 35- to 50-year-old man who may have been a ruler called Bird Jaguar. He died around A.D. 450, somewhat younger than many other Maya lords, who often lived to a ripe old age.

Bird Jaguar had not been in good health. He had injured his neck sometime before he died but had recovered from the trauma. The ruler wore a necklace of colored and matched apple-green jade. A vulture-headed jade pendant, symbol of Maya royalty, hung from it. A

*W*ritings and art from long ago hearken to life's intangible side. An 11th-century rune stone from Mariefred, southeastern Sweden, depicts a serpent. Using a 16-character alphabet designed for easy carving, rune masters limited their messages to bare facts and short verses. They often memorialized good works, long voyages, or tales of life and death. They afford tantalizing glimpses of the Viking age and its people.

hose move next? As a lion and an antelope sit down to a board game, hyenas and a cat herd gazelles and geese. While we can only guess what was on the artist's mind, this seemingly light-hearted bit of animal art from ancient Egypt may be a commentary on social chaos. Painted on papyrus sometime during the 20th or 21st Dynasty (1185 to 945 B.C.), it displays predators and prey in topsy-turvy roles—at a time when Egypt was in disarray. Tomb robbing raged unchecked, inflation ran rampant, and bandits roamed the land.

jade bead the size of a cherry lay in his mouth, perhaps serving as a receptacle for his spirit. His other grave goods, however, were rather poor, Hammond noted.

As far as we know, this Bird Jaguar was one of the first Maya rulers to receive a ceremonial burial. It seems to have been a hurried one, with few grave goods and a large but unmarked tomb. The lack of lavish adornments might be related to ongoing warfare that eventually led to the abandonment of La Milpa for more than two centuries.

Maya archaeologists are now working closely with epigraphers as they probe the secrets of Copan, Tikal, and other cities. Since 1980, teams from several American universities and the Honduras Institute of Archaeology and History have been investigating the complex history of what they call the Acropolis at Copan, the main political and religious precinct between A.D. 400 and 800. Like the Maya calendar and human existence itself, many Maya ceremonial buildings followed a cycle of ritual celebration, periodic renovation, and abandonment. They stood at intensely sacred locations that had been hallowed for generations; temple builders used the same sites again and again. The cycle began afresh when a new structure rose atop the old one, a construction technique that saved Maya architects a great deal of time and effort.

Obviously, we know late Maya architecture best, simply because the most recent structures are on the surface. Earlier palaces, pyramids, and temples lie beneath. To uncover them would require large-scale, destructive trenching: an ethically questionable strategy, especially in an era of threatened archaeological sites. But Copan is unique in that the nearby Río Copan has cut through the eastern edge of the Acropolis, revealing a 400-year layering of ancient buildings, one atop the next. This natural erosion allows archaeologists to tunnel into the core of the Acropolis, following plaza surfaces, walls, and other features buried under feet of compacted earth and rock fill.

Over the past ten years, a project directed by Robert Sharer, of the University of Pennsylvania Museum, has excavated nearly two miles of tunnels, exposing some four centuries of architectural history along the eastern part of the Acropolis. Unlike trenching, tunnel excavation does not disturb standing buildings. Yet it enables excavators to identify different

layers in the walls and floors of the tunnels, giving precise signposts to what was happening as buildings rose on the Acropolis. Using computer-based surveying stations, archaeologists can create three-dimensional plans of how those buildings changed over time.

Fortunately for modern archaeology, Maya rulers loved to exalt their architectural achievements and the accompanying rituals. On what archaeologists call "Altar Q," a critical inscription was found that serves as textual guide to the entire Copan dynasty. The glyphs, set down during the reign of the dynasty's 16th ruler, Yax Pasah (First Dawn), record the arrival of the founder Kinich Yax Kuk Mo (Sun-eyed Green Quetzal Macaw) in A.D. 426 and the 15 subsequent rulers who embellished and expanded the great city. Fortunately, too, Copan's Acropolis was a compact royal precinct, unlike Tikal or Palenque, where ceremonial and residential quarters were segregated. The archaeological tunnels at Copan have helped link various individual structures to the history of each of the city's identified rulers. Excavators also uncovered seven texts and their associated architecture. The earliest text dates to the reign of Copan's second ruler, allowing researchers to reconstruct a detailed history of the entire complex.

Erected in about A.D. 400, the earliest Acropolis buildings lie on a slight rise in a swampy area. Interestingly, glyph expert David Stuart has located a much later inscription that refers to the "place of reeds," a symbolic origin site for political institutions and early kings. The arrival of Kinich Yax Kuk Mo was marked by construction of a new Acropolis, which expanded rapidly and was a hive of continuous building activity until around A.D. 800. Its Late Classic period buildings are a final layer atop an earlier core.

Copan's earliest buildings fall into three separate political, ritual, and residential complexes, subsequently linked into a single Acropolis by A.D. 540. Just unraveling the complex histories of all the demolished buildings has taken years of excavation, survey, and analysis.

The core of the Acropolis evolved from a small masonry structure referred to by archaeologists as Hunal, its fine facade once decorated with brightly painted murals. Perhaps this was the residence of Kinich Yax Kuk Mo himself. Hunal stood on a low, plastered platform with at least four other adobe and masonry buildings. A vaulted tomb, built before the building was demolished, lies under Hunal's floor. It was first opened in

1996. Two years of consolidation and documentation will be needed to establish whether this is, indeed, the tomb of the founding dynast.

Hunal and its tomb became the sacred foundation for several temples built on the same site. During the mid-fifth century the second ruler—one of the founder's sons—promoted his father's dynastic status with a massive building program. He erected a funerary temple over Hunal, incorporating into the structure a vaulted tomb that could be accessed from later temples built at higher levels. Other new buildings arose, each more elaborate than its predecessor. The magnificent structure called Rosalila by its excavator, Honduran archaeologist Ricardo Agurcia Fasquelle, is Copan's only completely preserved building.

Eventually, an eminent person was buried in the vaulted tomb, one so important that veneration rituals were performed in the presence of the corpse on several occasions after the burial. At first, excavators assumed that the second ruler lay in the chamber. But physical anthropologist Jane Buikstra, of the University of New Mexico, identified the bones as those of an elderly woman. Perhaps she was a relative of Kinich Yax Kuk Mo, possibly the founder's wife. This discovery confirms the great importance of women in Maya political life and in the royal lineages that controlled Copan and other Maya kingdoms.

By constructing their own monuments atop the revered founder's tomb and ruined palace, Copan's lords provided a chronicle of royal power and dynastic politics, rooted firmly in a compelling symbolic world. Thanks to the surviving glyphs and to brilliant archaeology, Mayanists have opened the door to the richness of the ancient Maya world. Even now, we only partially understand its scope and subtleties.

Thousands of miles from Copan, one of archaeology's most dramatic discoveries of this century has required a very different decoding of the intangible. The Moche civilization of Peru's arid north coast flourished in one of the world's driest environments, from about A.D. 200 to 800. Its people were fisherfolk and irrigation farmers, expert hydraulic engineers and traders. They captured mountain runoff with elaborate canals and reservoirs that enabled them to raise plentiful crops of maize and cotton.

We know little of Moche society, but its rulers were powerful enough to command the labor of countless communities, and thus were able to construct great pyramids and temples. Until recently, the only clues we had to their identity were a series of finely sculpted pots bearing portraits of confident, serene individuals staring impassively into space.

In February 1987, looters from the village of Sipán in the Lambayeque Valley, some 420 miles northwest of Lima, broke into an adobe pyramid and found the previously undisturbed sepulchre of a Moche lord. When rumors of the find surfaced, the police contacted local archaeologist Walter Alva, director of the Bruning Museum in Lambayeque. He visited the tomb and at once realized its importance. Police armed with submachine guns guarded the archaeological site day and night, while Alva organized a rescue operation.

With the support of the National Geographic Society as well as other sources of funding, Alva and a team of young Peruvian archaeologists—assisted by Christopher Donnan of the University of California at Los Angeles—embarked on a systematic excavation of the looted tomb and the pyramid. Some idea of the richness of the original burial came from finds left undisturbed by the looters, including no less than 1,137 clay vessels, the largest offering of its kind ever found in the Americas.

When excavators unearthed the sepulchres of three men now known as the Lords of Sipán, they found elaborate regalia with all three, indicating that they had received very similar burial rites. Tomb I held the remains of a man who had died in his late 30s or early 40s. His brick burial chamber was deep within the pyramid, with solid mud-brick benches along the sides and head end. Hundreds of clay pots had been set in small niches in the benches. The dead lord wore a lavish costume and was arrayed with dazzling jewelry. He had been wrapped in textile shrouds and placed within a plank coffin in the center of the burial chamber. More ceramics had been laid at the foot and head of the coffin. Two llamas had been sacrificed and placed on either side at the foot of the coffin. Finally, the corpse of a nine- or ten-year-old child had been placed at the head of the nobleman.

Five cane coffins were in the grave, each containing an adult. Two were male. Possibly bodyguards or members of the lord's entourage, they also had been adorned, one with copper ornaments and a war club, the other with a beaded pectoral. Coffins containing two of the three women lay at the head of the royal casket; the third lay at the foot, the body turned on its side. The disarticulated and jumbled bones suggest that the women were not sacrificial victims but had died long before the lord and were partly decomposed at the time of his burial.

A beamed roof, too low for anyone to stand beneath, covered the burial chamber. Laborers had heaped basketfuls of earth over the timbers. A footless, sacrificial male occupied the fill. Another body, legs crossed, sat in a small niche in the south wall, about three feet above the roof.

A reconstruction of the royal regalia on a mannequin gives the impression of a powerful lord caparisoned in all his glory, as he might have appeared before the people on ceremonial occasions. The man in Tomb I wore a long tunic covered with platelets of gilded copper and hemmed with copper cones. Large, beaded bracelets of turquoise, shell, and gold adorned each wrist. A beaded pectoral, of gold and silver beads, covered his chest and shoulders. A waist belt supported bells and a golden backflap, which weighed nearly two pounds. A crescent-shaped gold ornament hung from his nasal septum, completely covering his mouth and the lower part of his face. Large ear ornaments inlaid with gold and turquoise hung from his ears.

Also in the coffin was a large crescent-shaped golden headdress ornament. The corpse held a gold-and-silver scepter in one hand, apparently an insignia of rank. The effect of such clothing and regalia must have been overwhelming in any public ceremony, as the lord's shining garments and ornaments gleamed in the bright sun. He might have assumed the splendor of a god.

Who was this Lord of Sipán? The Moche left no writings. Only their painted pots and sculptured vessels provide a record of individual lives and rulers.

Christopher Donnan has spent years creating a comprehensive photographic archive of surviving Moche pottery. Combing museums and private collections throughout the world, he has photographed the intricate paintings on hundreds of pots. He and his assistant Donna McClelland create "unrolled" views by taking multiple photographs of each pot and then drawing the designs, translating their curved surfaces to flat paper.

Often Donnan has found the same motif repeated on multiple pots. Some show Moche soldiers in ritual combat, charging opponents with clubs. The defenders raise feather-decked shields in defiance and attempt to capture the attackers. The Moche army prevails. Victors lead naked prisoners by ropes around their necks, the prisoners' weapons and clothing slung over their shoulders.

Other scenes depict sacrifices presided over by a warrior-priest, a large figure wearing regalia remarkably similar to those in the Sipán tombs. The victims have their throats cut and priests drink their blood; their body parts become display trophies. Donnan firmly believes that the individual in the principal tomb at Sipán was one of the very warrior-priests depicted on Moche vessels.

In the absence of recorded history, Moche scholars must rely on artifacts and regalia for information. Lavish use of gold and silver reflects the duality of sun and moon, as well as other ancient Andean beliefs. The intricate costume of each warrior-priest sent a potent message to his subjects. His surviving artifacts mirror such intangibles.

Few ancient societies offer testimonies of their past glory as vivid as Maya glyphs, Assyrian cuneiform, and Egyptian hieroglyphs. At most sites, the past comes alive through more prosaic material remains, perhaps a humble stone ax or rugged bronze sword. Only occasionally are we fortunate enough to find the spectacular artifacts of the mighty.

Today, we search for a deeper understanding of the intangibles of all human life. What fundamental beliefs compelled the Moche warrior-priests to conduct human sacrifices? Why and how did farmers at 'Ain Ghazal revere their ancestors? We live in a very different world from the ancients. Yet we must seek to understand them better—their drives, their emotions, their beliefs—if we are to apply the lessons of the past to future concerns.

E*nigmatic plaster figures (opposite), some with two heads, emerged en masse from a pit at 'Ain Ghazal, Jordan. Excavators removed them as a single unit, to minimize damage. Later, equipped with dental picks and strengthening chemicals, conservators at the Smithsonian Institution's Conservation Analytical Laboratory slowly "excavated" individuals from the cache. A xeroradiograph (below) reveals bundled reeds and twining that provide one figure's interior armature, around which plaster was molded. The 8,500-year-old figures—originally painted and probably clothed—now stare anew over the millennia. Carol Grissom reassembles the leg and torso of one serene ancestor (right).*

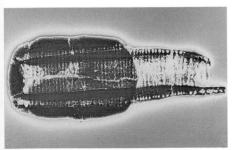

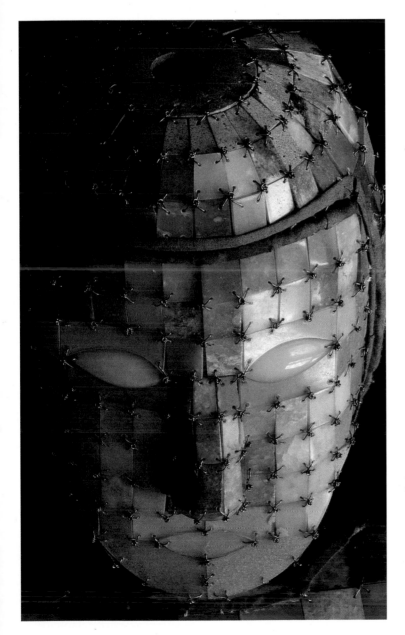

F aces from the past include a Teotihuacan-style stone mask inlaid with turquoise and shell (opposite). Found in Guerrero, Mexico, it testifies to the profound influence of Teotihuacan on distant Mesoamerican societies. Peaking at about 500 A.D., this great city rivaled Shakespeare's London in size; its pervasive beliefs and rituals spread throughout Mesoamerica.

Ancient Chinese nobles considered jade an armor against decay. In A.D. 90, local ruler Liu Yen was buried near Shijiazhuang, southwest of Beijing, in an elaborate funerary suit composed of hundreds of nephrite plates

joined with gold wire (left). The suit was to no avail, for excavators found no trace of his body.

Ancient Etruscans, however, cremated their dead, then memorialized the departed's likeness in clay. A crude but durable caricature—perhaps of the deceased—adorns an early Etruscan funerary urn (above).

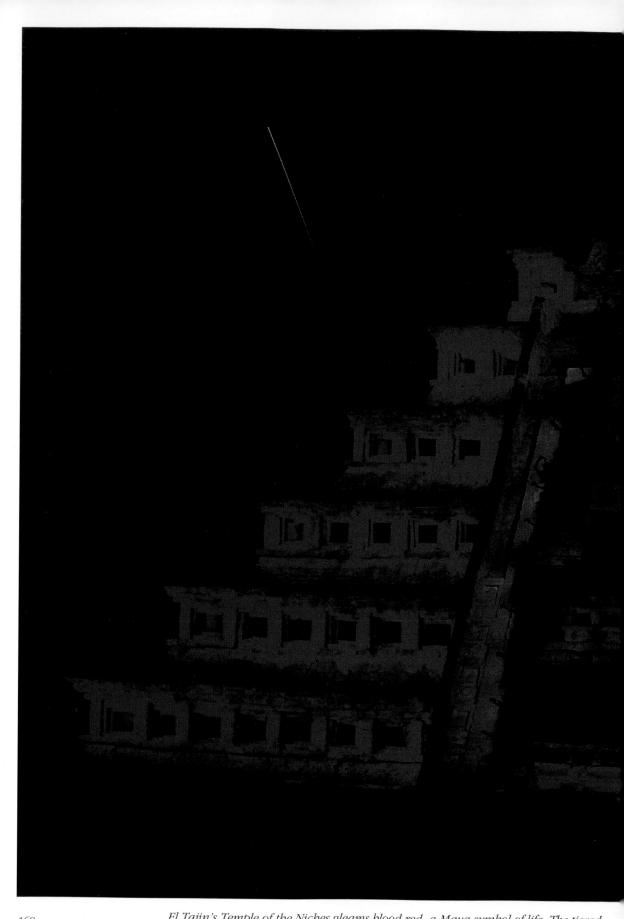

El Tajin's Temple of the Niches gleams blood red, a Maya symbol of life. The tiered

Mexican pyramid uses light-and-shadow contrasts with dramatic effect.

Celebrating the spring equinox, Mexican teams from Sinaloa breathe new life into the ancient ball court at Xochicalco, playing a game once immensely popular throughout Mesoamerica (bottom left). The court's sloping sides help keep the rubber ball in play as opponents try to knock it through a stone hoop without using their hands.

In antiquity, players often personified gods. The ritual ball game itself often meant life or death, since the leader of the losing team was decapitated and sacrificed to the gods. A cylindrical vessel probably from Campeche (above), depicts ballplayers and architectural elements of the ball court. "Unrolled" photographically by setting the vessel on a revolving platform, its complete image (opposite, top) reveals four players in black body paint, protected with deer-hide pads on one knee, foot, and wrist. A wood or wicker yoke tied under the arms provided additional protection as well as a striking surface to meet the ball.

rilliant colors and other details, unseen for centuries, glow anew in a computer-assisted reconstruction (left) of a faded Maya mural (below) at Bonampak, Mexico. The site's name stems from the Maya words for "painted wall." Here, incomparable murals adorn three rooms in a building on Bonampak's acropolis. Art historian Mary Miller believes the rooms relate a historical drama that serves as a window on the demise of the Classic Maya. Following a great dance in the first room, a grim battle in the second provides sacrificial victims; hard-eyed warriors surround the vanquished enemy. The third room shows Bonampak's noblewomen sealing an heir's right to the throne with a bloodletting ritual.

Miller and computer artist Doug Stern restore the image of a regal Bonampak lady (opposite, bottom). By using photographs that have been scanned into a computer and enhanced, they can discover long-obscured details. Trio of hands (bottom, left to right) takes on different manifestations in a color photograph, an infrared print, a tracing, and a composite, which reveals new details such as once hidden fingernails.

S easonal rhythms of planting and harvest still dominate the calendar in Mesoamerica, as they have for thousands of years. Guatemalan diviner Andrés Xiloj ponders seeds (opposite) and uses the 260-day Sacred Almanac of the Maya to determine auspicious dates. The Maya calendar served as a perpetual fortune-telling machine, with each day assigned various omens.

In Aztec myth and art, the first human couple (above) gathers in a sacred enclosure, casting corn-kernel lots to determine fates, while water beaded with droplets and shells flows out below. Like the Maya, Aztec priests used a 260-day calendar for rituals and omens; they even foretold the coming of the Spanish. In 1790, a carved basaltic disk depicting the Aztec cosmos (below left) was found in Tenochtitlan's main square— now Mexico City's Zócalo . A major god occupies the center, a sacrificial knife protruding from his mouth. Bas-reliefs in square panels refer to the passing of four previous Aztec "suns," or worlds, destroyed in turn by jaguars, wind, fiery rain, and water.

Colorful rendition by artist Felipe Dávalos (below), uses hues that likely adorned the stone originally. The design chronicles the ancient Aztec world and the arrival of the fifth sun, its flourishing, and its inevitable end.

Royal tombs of Sipán (left foreground), in Peru's Lambayeque Valley, were placed near

Moche pyramids of adobe brick, now so severely eroded that they resemble the Andean foothills. 177

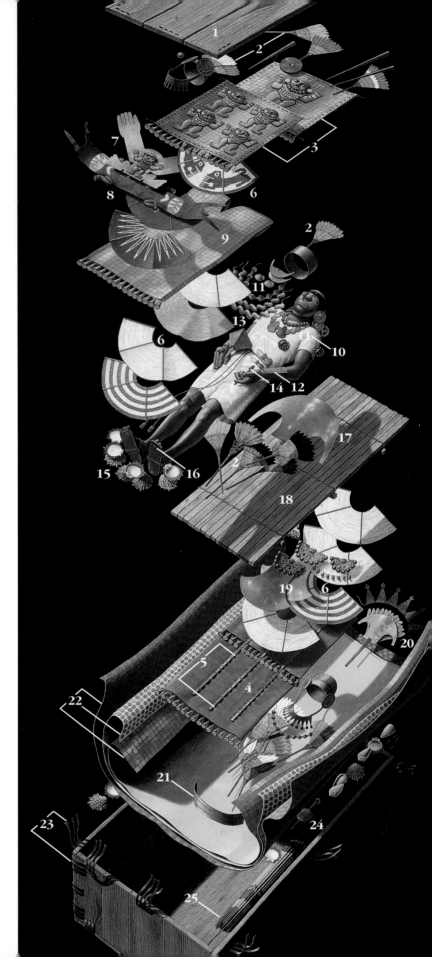

I ntact tomb at Sipán yielded the skeleton of a man who stood about five feet six inches tall—surrounded by various treasures. Beneath the coffin's lid (1), feather ornaments (2) occurred both above and below the body, as did fabric banners with gilded copper platelets (3,4). Copper struts (5) made the lower banners rigid. Also found: 11 chest coverings of shell and copper beads (6), a headdress of gilded copper (7), and a cloth headband (8). An outer shirt covered with gilded copper platelets (9) and a simple white garment (10) clothed the body, festooned with gold, silver, and copper ornaments (11). Turquoise and gold-bead bracelets adorned the forearms (12); the right hand held a gold scepter (13), the left a silver spatula (14). Seashells (15) lay at the sandaled feet (16).

Beneath the body, a massive gold headdress ornament (17) lay on a supporting wood frame (18). Underneath were gold bells, backflaps of gold and silver (19), and a small gold headdress ornament (20). The significance of copper strips (21) remains a mystery. Three shrouds (22) enfolded the contents of the coffin, which was bound with copper strapping (23). At the very bottom lay more shells, a miniature war club and shield (24), and copper-tipped atlatl darts (25).

Initial excavations revealed a royal individual amid exquisite funerary objects (opposite, top); workers slowly removed the many layers to expose the ruler's golden headdress (opposite, bottom).

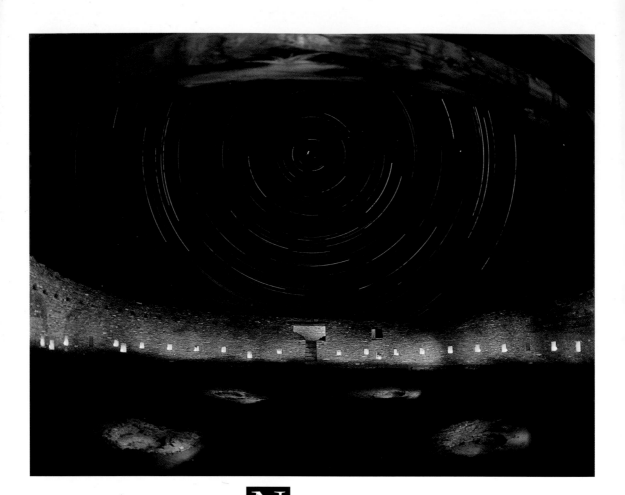

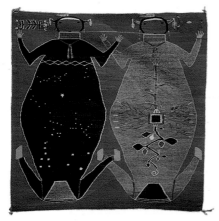

N atural or man-made, the sparkling dome of the southwestern sky once was vital to human existence. Stars wheel above the great kiva of Casa Rinconada at Chaco Canyon, New Mexico (above). As circular as the sky, the kiva reflects the astronomy of its Anasazi builders. Its main door faces celestial north. At dawn on the summer solstice, the sun's rays enter one window and strike a niche in the northwest wall, marking the sun's northernmost point on its yearly journey. Four lighted postholes mark where heavy pillars once stood, supporting the roof and defining the cardinal directions.

In Arizona's Canyon de Chelly National Monument, a "star ceiling" found by Navajo teacher Harry Walters shines down from the roof of a rock-shelter (opposite). Navajo mythology offers an explanation: Since stars hold up the sky, star symbols keep the rock ceiling from falling. Some Navajo believe the pictographs represent a hero who traveled to the heavens in search of ritual knowledge.

Two exact halves of the universe—Father Sky and Mother Earth—appear side by side in a nearly 60-year-old Navajo tapestry (left). Sacred plants grow upon Mother Earth, while stars and the Milky Way shine in Father Sky's domain.

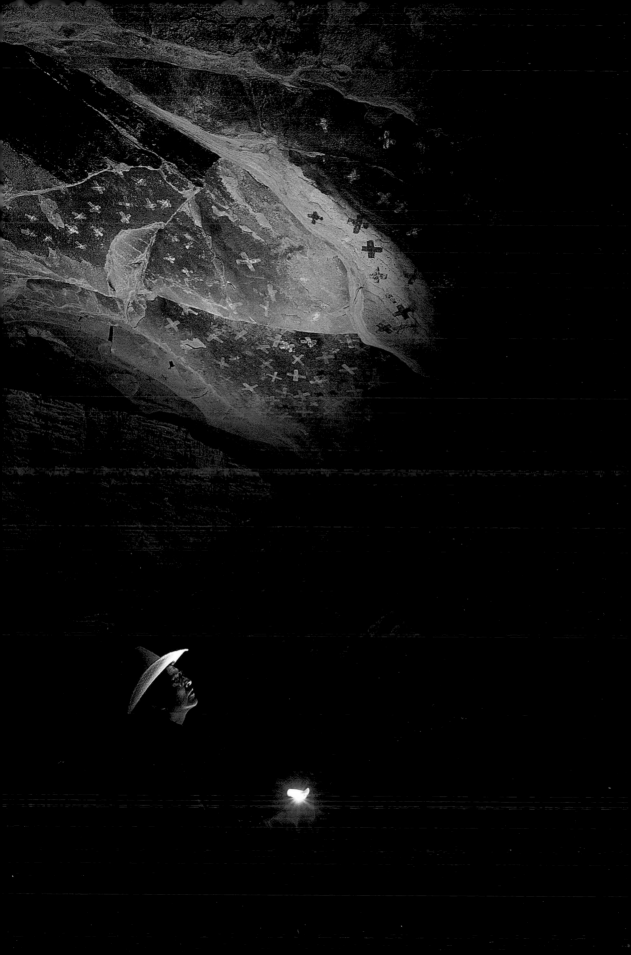

Seeking to look but not touch, scientists use a specially designed drilling system to examine

a funerary boat buried in an underground chamber beside the Great Pyramid of Khufu.

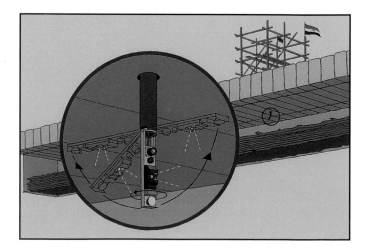

D ecades ago, Egyptian archaeologists excavated a 4,600-year-old funerary boat, built for Pharaoh Khufu and stored disassembled (above) in a pit near the Great Pyramid. It had been intended for Khufu's use in the afterlife. Eventually the 1,224 pieces of cedar were reconstructed into a 142-foot-long craft with a narrow beam and elegantly tapered stem and stern posts (top). Such "papyri-form" vessels were modeled on early papyrus watercraft.

Evidence of a second pit was noted during the original excavation. Archaeologists

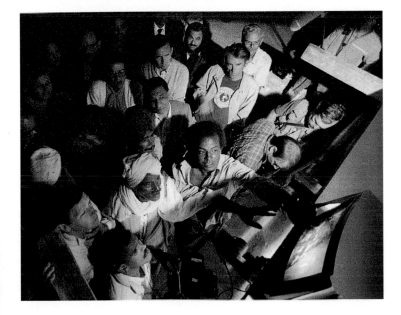

dreamed of peeking inside—but only if they would not damage the contents.

With help from the National Geographic Society, a rotating probe was rigged with strobe and viewing lights, as well as video and still cameras. On October 20, 1987 it was lowered into the chamber through a drilled hole that had been protected with an air lock (opposite, bottom). A video monitor enabled scientists and workers (left) to document that, as had been suspected, the chamber held a second boat.

riests of ancient Egypt chanted, "You will live again forever," as they embalmed the dead. Pharaohs and the wealthy paid large sums for mummification. In the catacombs (left) of Kom el-Shoqafa near Alexandria, priests in gods' masks begin to prepare a body for eternal life by removing the organs and embalming them in canopic jars.

Methods used at this second-century B.C. site had been refined over many centuries. Bodies were desiccated by packing them in salts, then treated with resin and wrapped in as many as 20 layers of linen.

According to the Greek historian Herodotus, ancient Egyptians showed crocodiles "every kindness." Mummified reptiles, crowded in a dark chamber at the Kom Ombo temple north of Aswan (opposite, bottom), honor crocodile-headed Sobek, deity of Nile fertility.

On a sepulchre wall at Thebes, weeping women mourn Ramose, vizier to two pharaohs, who died in the early 14th century B.C. Their ritualized gestures of mourning are remarkably similar to those of grieving villagers today. Ramose commissioned this funerary art at the height of his power.

"Possessor of charm, sweetness, and love," Pharaoh Ramses II proclaims his first and favorite wife, Nefertari, on a wall of her sepulchre in the Valley of the Queens, at Thebes. Her graceful and serene portrait (opposite, far left) adorns another wall. A devoted consort, she bore the pharaoh six or seven children before her death in about 1255 B.C.

Brightly painted guardians of the underworld watch over the central chamber of her tomb (above), but centuries of crystalizing salt have dislodged paint from the bedrock. Conservators from the Egyptian Antiquities Organization and the Getty Conservation Institute in Los Angeles have arrested the deterioration of the paintings.

Working with infinite patience, a conservator cleans a depiction of Nefertari in the presence of a goddess (opposite, right). Looters emptied the queen's richly painted sepulchre long ago, probably soon after her death, leaving almost nothing behind. Yet a fragment of a gold bracelet (right) came to light in the tomb as recently as 1987, a tantalizing memento of the staggering riches once buried with Ramses's beloved queen for her enjoyment in the afterlife.

Thanks to 20th-century computers, the Great Sphinx—a stone lion with the head of a pharaoh—reappears as "the living image of the sun god" (above). The Sphinx was built in about 2500 B.C. for King Khafre, builder of the second pyramid at Giza. Thutmose IV, son of Amenhotep II, freed the long-neglected Sphinx from blanketing desert sand around 1400 B.C., encasing its weathered body with limestone blocks, and painting it. He also may have erected a statue of his father in front of the Sphinx's chest.

Both Thutmose IV and Ramses II maintained the Sphinx as a shrine, now partly restored with fresh paws (top). Archaeologist Mark Lehner used photogrammetry and computers to create 3-D digital images of the Sphinx (right) he could manipulate to erase the effects of time. To reconstruct the original features of the Sphinx's face, Lehner drew from a life-size statue of Khafre (opposite, top).

Captured in nephrite for the ages, an Olmec shaman wears a duck mask, his animal

personality. Glyphs incised on head and body record a date equivalent to A.D. *162.*

INDEX

Boldface indicates illustrations

Abu Hureyra (site), Syria: ancient skeletons 26–27
Accelerator mass spectrometry (AMS) 28, **29,** 31, 154
Aerial photography 60, 62–63, **64,** 65, 68, **70,** 71
Agurcia Fasquelle, Ricardo 162
Ahmose I, Pharaoh (Egypt) 22
'Ain Ghazal (site), Jordan 165; plaster statues 11, **14–15,** 155–157, **164–165,** 165
Aitutaki Lagoon, Cook Islands: fisherman **142–143**
Akhenaten, Pharaoh (Egypt) 25, 39; bas-relief **38**
Alabama, C.S.S.: artifacts **132**
Altamira, Spain: cave art 151, 153–154
Altamura, Italy: Neandertal skeleton **34**
Alva, Walter 162
Amenhotep II, Pharaoh (Egypt) 190
Ampato, Nevado (peak), Peru: human sacrifice 48, **48–49**
Amun, Temple of, Jebel Barkal, Sudan: buried courtyard **80;** computer reconstruction **80–81**
Anasazi: astronomy 180, **180;** rock art **148–149**

Angkor Wat, Cambodia 70, 78, **79;** radar images 11, 70, **78**
Ankhensenpaaten, Queen (Egypt) 24, 25
Anorak, Inuit **44–45**
Apadana (audience hall), Persepolis, Iran: bas-relief **94–95**
Aramis, Ethiopia: hominid 19
Astronomy: Anasazi 180, **180;** Aztec 170, **170;** Maya 158; Navajo 180, **181**
Aubrey, John 61–62
Aufderheide, Arthur C. 28
Australopithecus afarensis **18,** 19; jaw **24;** model skull **195**
Avebury, England 66; stone circles 61, 62, 63
Aztec: calendar 88; carved stone **175;** cosmos stones **175;** farming 88; *see also* Teotihuacan

Ball court, Maya **170–171**
Bas-reliefs **36,** 37, **38,** 39, **94–95, 124–125**
Bass, George F. 96, 97, 108
Batoka Plateau, Zambia 91, 93
Beads: glass 11, 91, 93, 101, **114–115, 120;** gold 93
Bears 155; cave paintings 153, 154; fossils 153; hibernation 154; sculpture **102,** 103
Belderrig, Ireland 59, 61
Bison 155; cave paintings 154
Bonampak (site), Mexico: murals 10, **172–173,** 173
Bone diseases 25–27, 29, 32
Border Cave, South Africa: human fossils 19
Breadmaking **124–125,** 127, **138–139**
Bronze Age: artifacts 61; farms 59, 65, 66; excavations **76–77;** shipwrecks 11, 96–97, 106, 108; stone circles **64;** tools and weapons **77,** 108
Bronze artifacts **118–119**
Brothwell, Don 32
Brugsch, Emil 22
Brunel-Deschamps, Eliette 153, 154
Buikstra, Jane 162
Burial mounds 60–63, 99–100, 153
Byrne, Gretta 59

Çakir, Mehmet 96
Calakmul (site), Mexico 159

Camels **90–91;** bas-relief **94–95**
Campeche, Mexico: cylindrical vessel **170–171**
Cann, Rebecca L. 20, 21
Cano, Raúl J. 32
Canyon de Chelly National Monument, Ariz.: "star ceiling" 180, **181**
Caravan routes 91, 93, 101, 104
Casa Rinconada, Chaco Canyon, N. Mex. 180
Catherwood, Frederick 157–158
Caulfield, Patrick 59
Caulfield, Seamas 59, 60, 61
Cavalli-Sforza, Luigi Luca 19
Cave paintings **12, 148–151,** 153–155, **155,** 180, **181**
Cedar Mesa, Utah **148–149**
Céide Fields, County Mayo, Ireland: Stone Age farms 59–60, **60,** 61, 63, detection methods 57, 59, 60
Ceren, El Salvador 124, 127–128; serving dishes **127**
Chalcedony 99, 103
Chaplin, James 94
Chauvet, Grotte, France: cave paintings **150–151,** 153–154, **155**
Chauvet, Jean-Marie 153, 154
Cheyenne, Northern 132–133
Chinchorro culture: fishhooks **50;** mummies 50, **51**
Cleave, Richard 83
Cliff dwellings **148–149**
Clottes, Jean 154
Coins, bronze **121**
Colima culture 115; clay vessel **114,** 115
Collon, Dominique 97
Colono Ware 131–132
Computed tomography (CT) 23, 31, 34, **34,** 37, 48, **49**
Computers 10, 73; imagery **18,** 19, **35, 43,** 72, **73, 80–83,** **172–173,** 190; maps 71, 83
Copan (site), Honduras 66–69, 157–161; daily life **128,** 129
Copper 32–33, 94, 97, 99, 163; ax 30–32; frothing pot **110–111;** ingots 96–97, 106, **106,** 107; necklace 93; ornaments **178**
Cordy-Collins, Alana 115
County Kerry, Ireland: crop mark **64**
Cowgill, George L. 129

Archaeologists wait eagerly to investigate an Etruscan tomb under a highway at Tarquinia, Italy.

Crawford, O.G.S. 62
Cro-Magnons 153–155
Crocodiles: deity 187; mummified **186–187**
Cuello, Belize: trade goods **112**
Cunnington, William 63

Dagger, flint **47**; grass sheath **47**
Darwin, Charles 19
Deetz, James 132
Deir el-Bahari, Egypt: cache of mummies 22–23
Deir el-Balah (site), Gaza Strip 98, **99**
Dekin, Albert A., Jr. 28, 29
Diamonds: pendant **114–115**
Diving bell: replica **96**
DNA 17, 19, **24,** 31, 32, 39; *see also* Mitochondrial DNA
Documents, wooden 104, **105**
Dolmen **74–75**
Donnan, Christopher 162, 163, 164
Dothan, Trude 98
Drewitt, Bruce 129
Duch people (Egypt): bone diseases 25–26; laboratory analysis samples 25; X rays of mummies 25
Dunand, Françoise 25

Edwards, Amelia B. 22
Egg, Markus 32
El Mirador (site), Guatemala **86, 87**; topographical map **86–87**
El Tajin (site), Mexico 70; temple **168–169**
Endeavour (space shuttle): radar images 70, **78**
Ethiopia: discovery of hominids 19; hominid jaw **24**
Etowah, Georgia: rattle from burial mound **153**
Etruscans: cremation of dead 167; funerary urn **167**
Evans, John 65

Fan, turkey-feather **152, 153**
Fash, William L. 67
Ferguson, Leland 131
Fishing **142–143,** 143; fishhooks **50**; Roman mosaic depicting **142**; shellfishing 50
Flag Fen (site), England **76–77**; ancient timbers **76–77**; metal detectors **61**; transparent map **77**

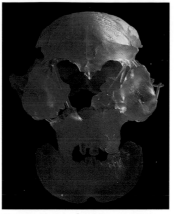

Computerized mirror imaging made possible this 3-D model, in plastic resin, of an **Australopithecus afarensis** *skull.*

Flenniken, J. Jeffrey 94
Florida: peat bog burial **30, 31**; seashells 99, 103
Freter, AnnCorinne 68
Frey, Donald A. 96
Funerary boats 182–183, **184–185**
Funerary suit, jade **167**
Funerary urn, Etruscan **167**

Gale, Noel 97
Genghis Khan 20; bronze plaque **21**
Geographic Information Systems (GIS) 11, 70–73
Giza, Pyramids of, Egypt 70, 91, 190
Glass: beads 11, 91, 93, 101, **114–115,** 115, **120**; ingots **108**; manufacturing process 108, **109**; *see also* Obsidian
Glyphs, Maya 4, **6–7,** 66, 157–159, 161, 162, 164
Goddio, Franck **111**
Godin Tepe, Iran 98
Golan Heights, Israel: stone circles **64**
Gold 97; beads 93; bracelet **189**; headdress **178–179**; Moche ceremonial regalia 163, **178–179**; pendants **106, 114–115**
Gould, Stephen Jay 21
Grisell, Bengt **96**
Grissom, Carol **165**
Guerrero, Mexico: stone mask **166,** 167
Gurche, John 19

Haifa, Israel: computer simula-

tion image **82–83**
Hall, John K. 83
Hammond, Norman 159
Hand stencils 154, **158**
Handt, Oliva 31
Harvest scenes: ancient Egypt **136–137**
Hawass, Zahi 127
Hillaire, Christian 153, 154
Hinduism 70, 78
Hoff, William C. 133
Homo sapiens sapiens 19
Hopewell culture 99–100; animal totems **102, 103**; burial mounds 99–100; earthwork **103**; trade 99, 103, map of trading routes **102**
Horses: cave paintings **150–151,** 153–154; skeletons 52, **53**
Human sacrifices **4–5,** 48, **48–49,** 163–165, 171, 173
Hunter-gatherers 17, 26, 155; peat burials **30, 31**
Huxley, Thomas Henry 19

Ice Age 59, 63, 151; art *see* Cave paintings
Ice Maiden (Inca mummy) **48–49**; clothing 48, **49**; 3-D image of skull 48, **49**
Iceman *see* Ötzi the Iceman
Indus Valley, Pakistan: miniature toys **136–137**
Ingombe Ilede, Mozambique 93, 94
Inuit: mummy of infant **44**; skeleton of woman **45**
Inupiat: frozen mummies 27–29
Isamu Pati, Zambia 91
Iskander, Nasry 24
Ivory 93, 108

Jade 93, 112, 160; funerary suit **167**; mosaic mask 159; Olmec statuette **192–193**
Jebel Barkal, Sudan: temple **80–81**
Jones, Andrew 31–32

Keiller, Alexander 62
Kelley, Jack 96
Kelso, William M. 131
Kendall, Timothy 80
Kenyon, Kathleen 157
Khafre, Pharaoh (Egypt) 190; diorite statue 190, **191**
Khmer Empire 70, 78

Khufu, Great Pyramid of, Giza, Egypt **182–183,** 185

Khufu, Pharaoh (Egypt): funerary boats **184–185,** 185

Kinich Yax Kuk Mo (Maya ruler) 67, 161, 162

Klasies River Mouth, South Africa: human fossils 19, 21

Knorozov, Yuri 158

Kom Ombo temple, Egypt: mummified crocodiles **186,** 187

Kom el-Shoqafa, Egypt: mummification rituals **186–187**

Kourion (site), Cyprus: bronze coins **121;** computer reconstruction of buildings 10; computer-generated map **43;** earthquake 43, **43;** skeletons **42,** 43

Kung San people **20**

Kush, Kingdom of 80; computer reconstruction of temples 10

La Milpa (site), Belize: burial chamber 159–160

Lambayeque Valley, Peru **176–177**

Landa, Diego de 158

Landsat images **71, 82–83, 86–87**

Lantos, Erzsebet 118, **119**

Lascaux, Montignac, France: cave paintings 153, 154

Lee, Daniel 86

Lehner, Mark 127, 190

Les Eyzies, France 153

Lewis, Kenneth E. 130

Lichtenberg, Roger 25

Lions: cave paintings **150–151,** 153–154, **155;** papyrus art **160**

Liu Yen: jade funerary suit **167**

Long barrows 62, 63, 64

Lopez, Santos **140–141**

Lounsbury, Floyd 159

Magnetometer surveys 10, 64, 65, 72

Maize: cultivation 70, 124, **140–141;** storage 149

Malinowski, Bronislaw 99

Mammoths: cave paintings 153, 154

Manzanilla, Linda 130, 146

Maspero, Gaston 22–23

Matheny, Ray T. 87

Matthews, Peter 159

Maudslay, Alfred Percival 158

Maya 59, 66–70, 86–87, 157–158, 160, 162; ball game **170–171;** calendar **174,** 175; daily life **128,** 129; farmer **140–141;** glyphs 4, **6–7,** 66, 157–159, 161–162, 164; human sacrifice 171, 173; royal burials 159–160; rulers 67, 159–162; temples 159, 162, **168–169;** trade goods **112;** vessels **112–113, 127, 170–171**

McGovern, Patrick E. 98

Mediterranean region: map of ancient trade routes 108–109; tsunami (A.D. 365) 43

Merchant's Barrio, Teotihuacan, Mexico **100,** 101

Mica 99, 103; carvings **102–103**

Middleburg Plantation, S.C. 131

Middleton Place, S.C. 130–131

Miller, Mary **172**

Millon, René 129

Mitochondrial DNA (mtDNA) 19–20, 23–25; diagram **24**

Moche culture 115, 162; burial **4–5;** human sacrifice 163, 165; pottery 162–164; *see also* Sipán

Mohawk: storyteller **152,** 153

Molleson, Theya 26, 27

Mongols 20, **21**

Monticello (estate), Va. 131, 133, **134–135,** 135

Moore, Andrew M. T. 26

Moore, Elizabeth 70

Moroz, Marina **54**

Mulberry Row, Monticello, Va. 131, 133, **134–135;** artifacts **133**

Mummies, Egyptian 22, **36;** blood lines 23–24, 39; DNA tissue analysis 24–25; x-ray examinations 23, 25

Murals **186–187;** computer-assisted reconstruction **172–173;** restoration **188,** 189

Naj Tunich (site), Guatemala: glyphs 4, **6–7**

Nakbe (site), Guatemala 86, **87**

Navajo: astronomy 180, **181;** pictographs 180, **181;** tapestry **180**

Nazca Lines **64**

Neandertals 19; computer reconstruction **35;** CT image of skull **34;** fossilized skeleton 34

Nefertari, Queen (Egypt) 24,

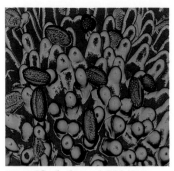

Magnified about 1,800 times, pollen grains on the stigma of sweet alyssum reveal their unique identity to botanists.

189; portrait **188;** tomb **188–189**

Nefertiti, Queen (Egypt) 97; bas-relief **38;** bust **39**

Nephrite: head of funerary suit **167;** statue **192–193**

Neumann, Paul 34, **35**

New Kingdom (Egypt) 23–24

Newark, Ohio: earthwork **103**

Nimrud, Assyria: palace 98

Nippur (ancient city), Sumer: excavations **8–9**

Niya (ancient city), Xinjiang, China: bowl **104;** door carvings **104;** ruins 104, **104–105;** wooden documents 104, **105**

Nuestra Señora de la Concepción (ship): treasure **114–115**

Obsidian 112; arrowhead **113;** blades 94; dating 68; Maya mirror 10; spear points 103; trade in 68, 94–95, 99

Oglala Sioux: shell dress **121**

Olmec: nephrite figure of shaman **192–193**

Otstungo (site), New York: Mohawk longhouse **152,** 153

Ötzi the Iceman 10, 29, **46, 47,** 48; clothing 31–33, 37; corpse **46, 47;** diseases 31–32; implements 30–33, **47**

Oztoyahualco, Teotihuacan, Mexico 130; apartment compound **146–147**

Pacal the Great (Maya ruler) 159

Palenque (site), Mexico 66, 158–159, 161

Pandora, H.M.S.: excavation **97**

Panum Crater, Inyo National

Forest, Calif. **113;** obsidian 113
Papyrus art **160–161**
Pastron, Allen G. 133
Pazyryk people: mummy of
  woman 52, **54–55;** sacrifical
  horses 52, **53;** tomb **52–53**
Peat 57, 59, 60; ancient brain
  found in **30,** 31; burials **30,** 31;
  tephra deposits 61
Pendants, gold **106, 114–115**
Pendleton, Michael 98
Persepolis, Iran: bas-relief **94–95**
Petrie, Flinders 23
Piedras Negras (site), Guatemala
  158–159
Pinturas, Río, Argentina:
  rock art **158**
Platzer, Werner 31
Polosmak, Natalya 52
Porcelain, Chinese **111**
Pottery making **126,** 127
Poulnabrone dolmen, Ireland
  74–75
Proskouriakoff, Tatiana 158–159
Pryor, Francis 61, 65, 66, **76**
Puabi, Queen (Sumeria) 10
Pulak, Cemal 96, 97, 98, 108
Pyramid of the Moon, Teotihua-
  can, Mexico 129, **144–145**
Pyramid of the Sun, Teotihua-
  can, Mexico **84–85, 100,** 129,
  144–145
Pyrénées (mountains), France-
  Spain: cave paintings 153

Qilakitsoq, Greenland:
  Inuit mummy **44;** skeleton
  of woman **45**
Qin Shihuang, Emperor (China):
  terra-cotta army **40–41**
Qurna, Egypt: aerial
  view **2–3**

Radar imagery 11, **58,**
  59, 69–70, **71, 78**
Radiocarbon dating
  28, 60, 61, 66,
  68, 154
Ramose, vizier
  (Egypt) 187
Ramses II, Pharaoh
  (Egypt) 22, 36, 81,
  189, 190; diseases 23,
  37; entrance to
  tomb **36,** 37; mummy
  36
al-Rassoul brothers 22

Rattray, Evelyn 101
Redding, Martin **77**
Reinhard, Johan 48
Renfrew, Colin 95
Rhinoceroses: cave paintings
  153, 154
Robinson, Mark 66
Rollefson, Gary 156
Rome, ancient 118; fishing 143;
  Mithraic worship 104; mosaic
  142; silk cultivation 93; toga-
  clad statue **116–117**
Rouse, Amanda 65
Rub al Khali (Empty Quarter),
  Arabian Peninsula: radar images
  69, **71**
Rune stone (Viking): Mariefred,
  Sweden **159**
Ruz Lhuillier, Alberto 159

San Diego (ship): stoneware jar
  111; wreck 111
San Francisco, Ca.: excavation of
  store 133
Sanders, William T. 67
Santa Luisa, Veracruz, Mexico:
  aerial photograph **70**
Sauneron, Serge 25
de Sautuola, Don Marcelino
  Sanz 151, 153
Scanning electron microscopes
  27, 98
Schele, Linda 159
Seidler, Horst 32
Seqenenre II, Pharaoh (Egypt)
  23
Seti I, Pharaoh (Egypt): mummy
  22, 23
Sharer, Robert 160
Sheets, Payson 127

Shells 11, 103, 112, 153, 163,
  178, **179;** armband **121;** *Conus*
  93; *dentalium* **120–121;** dress
  121; fishhooks 50; headdress
  120, 121; *kula* 99, **121,** 123;
  mother-of-pearl bowl **110,** 111;
  mussel **50**
Shield Jaguar (Maya ruler) 159
Shipwrecks 11, 96–98, 106, 115,
  132; cargo 97, 98, **106–107,**
  108, **110–111, 114–119;**
  Spanish galleons 111, 115
Shisur (site), Oman 69, 71
Silk: 18th-century waistcoat **92,**
  93; trade 91, 93, 104
Silk Road, Asia 91, 104
Silver 163, 165; ornaments **178;**
  pitcher and spoon **110,** 111
Simmons, Alan 156
Simon, Helmut and Erika 30
Sinaloa (state), Mexico: ball
  players **170–171**
Single-laser-fusion dating 24, **24**
Sipán (site), Peru 162–165;
  tombs **4–5, 176, 178–179**
Slaves, African-American
  130–133
Smoke Shell (Maya ruler) 67
Spectrographic analysis 11, **94**
Spence, Michael 101
Sphinx, Giza, Egypt:
  3-D digital images 190,
  190–191; restoration **190**
Spindler, Konrad 30, 31, 33
Stein, Sir Aurel 104
Stelae 157–159
Stephens, John Lloyd 157, 158
Stern, Doug **172**
Stonehenge, England **56–57**
Stoneking, Mark 20, 21
  Stone mask, Teotihuacan
  style **166**
Stuart, David 161
  Suryavarman II, King
  (Khmer Empire) 78

Ta-Bes (Egyptian
  mummy): CT scanner
  37; image **37**
Tajiks: young girl
  16–17
Tassili-n-Ajjer, Algeria
  12–13, 13; cave
  painting **12**
Taylor, Maisie **77**
Temple of the
  Inscriptions, Palenque,

Travesty of modern-day vandalism defaces an elk painted perhaps 1,600 years ago by the Fremont people in a small cave in Nine-Mile Canyon, Utah.

Enclosed in sandstone brought from dozens of miles away, 1,500-year-old burial urns attributed to the little-known Ngorek people stud the Borneo forest. The burial chambers remain a mystery.

Mexico 159
Temple of the Niches, El Tajin, Mexico **168–169**
Tenochtitlan: carved Aztec stone **175**
Teotihuacan, Mexico 67, **84–85,** 101, 129–130, **144–145,** 167; apartment **146–147;** barrios **100,** 101, 129–130, 146
Thebes, Egypt 22, 81, 101; City of the Dead **2–3;** mural of funerary scene **187**
Thutmose II, Pharaoh (Egypt) 81
Thutmose III, Pharaoh (Egypt) 22
Thutmose IV, Pharaoh (Egypt) 190
Tigre Pyramid, El Mirador, Guatemala 87
Tikal (site), Guatemala 66, 159–161
Tiy, Queen (Egypt) 24, 25, 39; bust **38**
Tlingit: headdress **120,** 121
Toldense people: handprints **158**
Tomb paintings **1, 106–107, 187**
Trade 68–69, 93–99, 101, 103–104, 106–108, 111–112, 115–116, 118, 121, 123; maps of routes 102, 108–109

Trobriand Islands, South Pacific Ocean: kula shell trade 99, 123; outrigger canoe **122–123**
Turquoise 163, 167; mask **166**
Tutankhamun, Pharaoh (Egypt): blood lines 39; bust **38;** dissection of mummy 23; funerary bed 97
Tuthmosis I, Pharaoh (Egypt) 23
Tuthmosis IV, Pharaoh (Egypt) 23

Ugarit (ancient port), Syria 97
Ukok Plateau, Russia 52, **52–53**
Uluburun, Turkey 99; shipwreck 11, 96, 106, 108
Underwater archaeology **96–97, 106, 111, 116–117**
Ur, Mesopotamia 8, 10
Utqiagvik (site), Alaska 28–29
Uxmal (site), Mexico 158

Valley of the Kings, Egypt 22
Valley of the Queens, Egypt 189
Viroconium Cornoviorum (Roman town), Wroxeter, England 11, 71–73
Voigt, Mary M. 98
Volcanic eruptions 61, 124, 125

Walters, Harry 180, **181**

Ward, Cheryl Haldane 98
Warnock, Peter 98
Ways of Horus (trading route) 98
Webster, David 67
Weiher, Wendy **58,** 59
White, Tim 19
Whittle, Alasdair 64
Willey, Gordon R. 67
Wilson, Allan C. 19–21
Winemaking 98, 99
Woodward, Scott 24
Woolley, C. Leonard 8, 10
Wroxeter, England 11, 71–73

X rays 23, 25, 31, 33, 37, 45
Xochicalco (site), Mexico: ball court **170–171**
Xochimilco, Mexico City, Mexico: floating gardens **88–89**

Yax Pasah (Maya ruler) 67, 161
Yaxchilan (site), Mexico 159

Zambezi Valley, Africa 93
Zapotitan Valley, El Salvador 124, 127
Zárate, Miguel **48**
Zimmerman, Larry 133
Zimmerman, Michael R. 28

ILLUSTRATIONS CREDITS

FRONTMATTER: 1 Art Resource, N.Y.; 2-3 O. Louis Mazzatenta; 4-5 Kevin Schafer/Tony Stone Images; 6-7 Wilbur E. Garrett

INTRODUCTION: 8-9 The University Museum, Philadelphia; 12-13 Kazuyoshi Nomachi/Pacific Press Service; 14-15 John Tsantes/Smithsonian Institution

PEOPLE OF THE PAST: 16-17 Reza; 18 Enrico Ferorelli; 20 Anthony B. Bannister; 21(both) James L. Stanfield; 24(T) Enrico Ferorelli, 24(BL) Carlyn Iverson, courtesy *Archaeology Magazine*; 24(BR) Enrico Ferorelli; 29 James King Holmes/Science Photo Library/Photo Researchers; 30(T) Glen H. Doran, Windover Archaeological Research Project; 30(B) William H. Bond; 34(BL) Soprintendenza Archeologica della Puglia; 34(T & BR) Kenneth Garrett; 35(T) Data for reconstructions from Natural History Museum, London; University of Zürich; and Cyberware; 35(B) Kenneth Garrett; 36(both) O. Louis Mazzatenta; 37(both) Alexander Tsiaras/ Science Source/Photo Researchers; 38(TL) Fred Maroon; 38(TR&B) Victor R. Boswell, Jr.; 39(L) Victor R. Boswell, Jr.; 39(R) C. Wilfred Griggs; 40-41 O. Louis Mazzatenta; 42 Martha Cooper; 43(T) Paintings by Bryn Barnard; 43(T) Graphics by Davis Meltzer; 43(B) Martha Cooper; 44(T) Jens P. Hart Hansen, Jørgen Meldgaard, and Jørgen Nordqvist; 44(B) John Lee/National Museum, Copenhagen; 45(both) Jens P. Hart Hansen, Jørgen Meldgaard, and Jørgen Nordqvist; 46 Sygma; 46-47 Kenneth Garrett; 47(T) S. Elleringmann/Bilderberg/ Aurora; 47(B) Kenneth Garrett; 48 Johan Reinhard; 48-49 Stephen Alvarez; 49(T) Christopher A. Klein, NGS 49(B) Johns Hopkins Hospital; 50-51(all) Enrico Ferorelli; 52 Charles O'Rear; 52-53 Charles O'Rear; 53(TL) Drawing by Yelena Shumakova & William H. Bond; 53(TR) Charles O'Rear/Westlight; 54-55 Charles O'Rear

ANCIENT LANDSCAPES: 56-57 Joseph Drivas/The Image Bank; 58 Kenneth Garrett; 60 Department of Arts, Culture and the Gaeltacht, Ireland, Céide Fields, County Mayo; 61 Adam Woolfitt; 64(T) Duby Tal & Moni Haramatti/Masa Archer Magazine, Tel Aviv; 64(BL) Robert Frerck/Tony Stone Images; (BR) Georg Gerster/Comstock; 70 S. Jeffrey K. Wilkerson; 71 USGS/Science Photo Library/Photo Researchers; 73 W. Fredrick Limp, Center for Advanced Spatial Technologies, University of Arkansas; 74-75 Ron Sanford/Tony Stone Images; 76-77(all) Adam Woolfitt; 78 NASA; 79 Nihon Denpa News, Ltd.; 80(T) Timothy Kendall; 80(B) Computer image by Susanne Gänsicke, Kevin Smith, and William Riseman; 80-81 Computer image by Susanne Gänsicke, Kevin Smith, and William Riseman; 82-83(all) Richard Cleave and Technion (Israel Institute of Technology); 84-85 Kenneth Garrett; 86 Terry W. Rutledge; 86-87 Landsat 5 Thematic Mapper, John C. Stennis Space Center, NASA; 87 Kenneth Garrett; 88-89 Stuart Franklin

WEBS OF COMMERCE: 90-91 Guido Alberto Rossi/The Image Bank; 92 Cary Wolinsky; 94-95 George Holton/Photo Researchers; 96 Bill Curtsinger; 97 Ben Cropp; 99 Lloyd K. Townsend; 100 Chuck Carter; 102(B) Richard Alexander Cooke, III; 103(both) Richard Alexander Cooke, III; 104(T&M) Reza/Hotan Museum; 104-105(T&B) Reza; 105(B) Reza/Hotan Museum; 106 (L) Donald Frey; (R) Bill Curtsinger; 106-107 Ned & Rosalie Seidler; 107 Bill Curtsinger; 108(both) Bill Curtsinger; 109 Terry W. Rutledge; 110 Jonathan Blair; 111(T) Emory Kristof;

111(B) Jonathan Blair; 112 Martha Cooper/Peter Arnold, Inc.; 112-113 University of Pennsylvania, Philadelphia; 113(both) James L. Amos; 114(B) University of Colima; 114-115(T) Sisse Brimberg; 114-115(B) David L. Arnold, 115 O. Louis Mazzatenta; 116-117 N. Lamboglia Underwater Research Group, Provincial Archaeological Museum, Brindisi; 118-119 O. Louis Mazzatenta/ Soprintendenza Archeologica della Puglia; 119 O. Louis. Mazzatenta/Istituto Centrale del Restauro, Rome; 120 Victor R. Boswell, Jr.; 121(T) Edward S. Curtis; 121(M) Martha Cooper/ Peter Arnold, Inc.; 121(B) Peter Essick/ Aurora; 122-123 Peter Essick/Aurora

LIVES OF THE HUMBLE: 124-125 Kenneth Garrett; 126 Kenneth Garrett; 127 Payson D. Sheets; 128 Tom H. Hall; 132 Olivier Pohu Archéolyse International; 133 & 134-135 Thomas Jefferson Memorial Foundation; 136 Joseph J. Scherschel; 136-137(T) Victor R. Boswell, Jr. from *Ancient Egyptian Paintings* by Nina M. Davies and Alan H. Gardiner, courtesy The Oriental Institute, University of Chicago; 136-137(B) Museum of Fine Arts, Boston; 138-139 Richard T. Nowitz; 140-141 David Alan Harvey; 142 Jonathan Blair/ Museum of Antique Art, Sousse; 142-143 Nicholas DeVore III; 144-145 Kenneth Garrett; 146 Kenneth Garrett; 146-147 Chuck Carter; 148-149 Fred Hirschmann

MIRRORS OF THE INTANGIBLE: 150-151 Jean-Marie Chauvet/Sygma; 152 Jack Unruh; 153 Lynn Johnson; 155 Jean-Marie Chauvet/Sygma; 158 François Gohier/Photo Researchers; 159 Kevin Schafer/Peter Arnold, Inc.; 160-161 Brian Brake/ British Museum/Photo Researchers; 164-165(all) courtesy Carol Grissom/Smithsonian Institution; 166 Kenneth Garrett/Museo Nacional de Antropología, Instituto Nacional de Antropología e Historia, Mexico City; 167(L) Fred Ward/Hebei Provincial Museum, Shijiazhuang, China; 167(R) O. Louis Mazzatenta/ Archaeological Museum, Siena; 168-169 David Hiser; 170(T) & 171(T) Justin Kerr/Dallas Museum of Art, Gift of Patsy R. and Raymond Nasher; 170-171 Bob Sacha; 172 Chris Johns, NGP; 172-173 Doug Stern; 173(T & BL) Enrico Ferorelli; 173(BML) Giles Healy; 173(BMR & BR) Doug Stern; 174 Bob Sacha; 175(T) Borbonicus Codex, Bourbon Palace, Paris/Time Inc.; 175(BL) Harald Sund/The Image Bank; 175(BR) Felipe Dávalos; 176-177 Bill Ballenberg; 178 Ned Seidler; 179(T) Heinz Plenge; 179(B) Martha Cooper; 180-181(all) Bob Sacha; 182-183 James P. Blair; 184 Pierre Mion; 184-185(T) Victor R. Boswell, Jr.; 184-185(M) Hag Ahmed Yousef; 185 Wilbur E. Garrett; 186 Nick Nicholson/The Image Bank; 186-187 David W. Hamilton/ The Image Bank; 187 George Holton/Photo Researchers; 188(BL&BR) O. Louis Mazzatenta; 188-189 O. Louis Mazzatenta; (189) Guillermo Aldana E./Getty Conservation Institute; 190(T) O. Louis Mazzatenta; (B) William H. Bond; 191(T) O. Louis Mazzatenta/Egyptian Museum, Cairo; 191-192(T&B) The National Geographic sponsored this modeling of the Sphinx. Architect Jon Jerde contributed computer facilities at Jerde Partnership Inc., of Venice, California. Tom Jaggers, director of computer-aided design, digitized maps drawn by Mark Lehner and by Ulrich Kapp of the German Archaeological Institute to create the model. The Sphinx mapping was sponsored in part by the American Research Center in Egypt and supervised by the Egyptian Antiquities Organization. 192-193 Kenneth Garrett/ Smithsonian Institution, Dumbarton Oaks Collection.

BACKMATTER: 194 O. Louis Mazzatenta; 195 Enrico Ferorelli; 196 David Scharf/Peter Arnold, Inc.; 197 Fred Hirschmann; 198 Eugene Fisher, 200 Otis Imboden and Emory Kristof/ Smithsonian Institution, Dumbarton Oaks Collection.

AUTHOR'S NOTE

British-born BRIAN FAGAN, one of the world's most prolific archaeological writers, studied archaeology at Cambridge University and spent his early career at the Livingstone Museum in central Africa, where he excavated Iron Age villages in what is now southern Zambia. Since 1967, he has been Professor of Anthropology at the University of California, Santa Barbara. A former Guggenheim Fellow and well-known lecturer, he has written numerous popular books on archaeology, including *The Rape of the Nile*, an award-winning account of early Egyptology, also the National Geographic Society's *The Adventure of Archaeology* and *Time Detectives*. He is a Contributing Editor to *Archaeology* magazine and has also written widely for specialist and general periodicals. His main archaeological interest is the impact of science on the study of humanity. An enthusiastic cruising sailor, Mr. Fagan also loves bicycling, cats, kayaking, and fine dinner parties.

ACKNOWLEDGMENTS

The Book Division wishes to thank the many individuals, groups, and organizations mentioned or quoted in this publication for their help and guidance. In addition, we are grateful to the following:

Neville Agnew, The Getty Conservation Institute; Ghazi Bisheh, Ministry of Tourism and Antiquities, The Hashemite Kingdom of Jordan; Edward Bleiberg, University of Memphis; Ros Cleal, Alexander Keiller Museum; Lyn Clement; Glen H. Doran, Florida State University; Mary Hardin, Jet Propulsion Laboratory; Carolinda E. Hill; Marie Jarin, France Office, National Geographic Society; Donald C. Johanson, Institute of Human Origins, Arizona State University; W. Fredrick Limp, University of Arkansas; William D. Lipe, Washington State University; Byron Loubert, Earth Satellite Corporation; Valerie Mattingley, United Kingdom Office, National Geographic Society; O. Louis Mazzatenta; Bonnie Morrow; Martha Potter Otto, Ohio Historical Society; Claude E. Petrone; Martijn van Leusen, The Wroxeter Hinterland Project; Ann Wise; Juris Zarins, Southwest Missouri State University.

Composition for this book by the National Geographic Society Book Division. Printed and bound by R. R. Donnelley & Sons, Willard, OH. Color separations by North American Color, Inc., Portage, MI; Phototype Color Graphics, Pennsauken, NJ. Dust jacket printed by Miken Companies, Inc., Cheektowaga, NY.

Visit the Society's Web site at **www.nationalgeographic.com.**

ADDITIONAL READING

The reader may wish to consult the *National Geographic Index* for related articles and books. The following sources may also be of interest: Brian Fagan, *Time Detectives*; Colin Renfrew and Paul Bahn, *Archaeology: Theories, Methods, and Practice*; Roger Lewin, *The Origin of Modern Humans*; Konrad Spindler, *The Man in the Ice*; Peter A. Clayton, *Chronicle of the Pharaohs: The Reign by Reign Record of the Rulers and Dynasties of Ancient Egypt*; Françoise Dunand and Roger Lichtenberg, *Mummies: A Voyage Through Eternity*; Caroline Malone, *English Heritage Book of Avebury*; Francis Pryor, *English Heritage Book of Flag Fen: Prehistoric Fenland Centre*; Geoffrey Wainwright, *The Henge Monuments: Ceremony and Society in Prehistoric Britain*; Donald N. Wilber, *Persepolis: The Archaeology of Parsa, Seat of the Persian Kings*; Payson D. Sheets, *The Ceren Site: A Prehistoric Village Buried by Volcanic Ash in Central America*; David Soren and Jamie James, *Kourion: The Search for a Lost Roman City*; Leland Ferguson, *Uncommon Ground: Archaeology and Early African America, 1650-1800*; Kathleen Berrin and Esther Pasztory, eds., *Teotihuacan: Art from the City of the Gods*; Michael D. Coe, *The Maya*; William L. Fash, *Scribes, Warriors and Kings: The City of Copán and the Ancient Maya*; Linda Schele and Mary Ellen Miller, *The Blood of Kings: Dynasty and Ritual in Maya Art*; Jean-Marie Chauvet, Eliette Brunel-Deschamps, and Christian Hillaire, *Dawn of Art: The Chauvet Cave*; Walter Alva and Christopher B. Donnan, *Royal Tombs of Sipán*; Christopher B. Donnan, *Moche Art of Peru*.

Library of Congress Cataloging-in-Publication Data

Fagan, Brian M.
    Into the unknown : solving ancient mysteries / by Brian Fagan.
       p.   cm.
    "Prepared by the Book Division, National Geographic Society, Washington, D.C."
    Includes bibliographical references and index.
    ISBN 0-7922-3653-X (reg.) —ISBN 0-7922-4233-5 (dlx)
    1. Archaeology—History. 2. Archaeology—Methodology.
3. Archaeology—Technological innovations. 4. Antiquities.
5. Civilization, Ancient. 6. Prehistoric peoples. I. National Geographic Society (U.S.). Book Division. II. Title.
CC100.F34 1997
930—dc21   97—23153
                                    CIP
                                    r97

Rollout photograph of a Maya cylindrical vessel dating to the eighth century A.D. *depicts a Maya ruler staring into an obsidian mirror in his role as "the mirror in which people see themselves."*